Summary of the History and Development of Mediaeval and Modern European Music

CHARLES HUBERT HASTINGS PARRY

CAMBRIDGE UNIVERSITY PRESS

Cambridge, New York, Melbourne, Madrid, Cape Town, Singapore,
São Paolo, Delhi, Dubai, Tokyo

Published in the United States of America by Cambridge University Press, New York

www.cambridge.org
Information on this title: www.cambridge.org/9781108005159

© in this compilation Cambridge University Press 2009

This edition first published 1893
This digitally printed version 2009

ISBN 978-1-108-00515-9 Paperback

This book reproduces the text of the original edition. The content and language reflect the beliefs, practices and terminology of their time, and have not been updated.

Cambridge University Press wishes to make clear that the book, unless originally published by Cambridge, is not being republished by, in association or collaboration with, or with the endorsement or approval of, the original publisher or its successors in title.

CAMBRIDGE LIBRARY COLLECTION

Books of enduring scholarly value

Music

The systematic academic study of music gave rise to works of description, analysis and criticism, by composers and performers, philosophers and anthropologists, historians and teachers, and by a new kind of scholar - the musicologist. This series makes available a range of significant works encompassing all aspects of the developing discipline.

Summary of the History and Development of Mediaeval and Modern European Music

In 1893, the English composer and director of the Royal College of Music C. Hubert H. Parry published Summary of the Development of Medieval and Modern European Music, an overview of European music from the middle ages to the work of Schubert and Brahms. Intended for music students, the book summarises the major composers, their work and the social circumstances that surrounded the creation of their music. This ambitious book is divided into 12 chronological chapters, from the troubadours and plainsong, through Bach and Handel to the rise of the symphony, Mozart, and the emergence of music as an expression of nationalism. In the book's first part, Parry deftly puts music in historical context, discussing England's Wars of the Roses, and the Reformation in relation to the changing styles throughout the sixteenth century; he then explores the music of the Restoration and the rise of opera.

Cambridge University Press has long been a pioneer in the reissuing of out-of-print titles from its own backlist, producing digital reprints of books that are still sought after by scholars and students but could not be reprinted economically using traditional technology. The Cambridge Library Collection extends this activity to a wider range of books which are still of importance to researchers and professionals, either for the source material they contain, or as landmarks in the history of their academic discipline.

Drawing from the world-renowned collections in the Cambridge University Library, and guided by the advice of experts in each subject area, Cambridge University Press is using state-of-the-art scanning machines in its own Printing House to capture the content of each book selected for inclusion. The files are processed to give a consistently clear, crisp image, and the books finished to the high quality standard for which the Press is recognised around the world. The latest print-on-demand technology ensures that the books will remain available indefinitely, and that orders for single or multiple copies can quickly be supplied.

The Cambridge Library Collection will bring back to life books of enduring scholarly value (including out-of-copyright works originally issued by other publishers) across a wide range of disciplines in the humanities and social sciences and in science and technology.

NOVELLO, EWER AND CO.'S MUSIC PRIMERS.

Edited by Sir JOHN STAINER.

SUMMARY

OF THE

HISTORY AND DEVELOPMENT

OF

MEDIÆVAL AND MODERN

EUROPEAN MUSIC

BY

C. HUBERT H. PARRY.

PRICE TWO SHILLINGS.
In paper boards, Two Shillings and Sixpence.

LONDON & NEW YORK
NOVELLO, EWER AND CO.

PREFACE.

A FAIRLY comprehensive and orderly understanding of the history of his art is of great importance to a musician, both for the light it throws upon every department of practical work, for the widening of his artistic sympathies, and for the service that a rational study of history of any kind is capable of rendering to a man's mind and judgment.

History is generally supposed to be based on facts; but in all branches, whether political, social, or artistic, there are a great many things which pass for facts which are very far from trustworthy, and a great many which, even if they were trustworthy, would be of very little importance.

The personal details of the lives of men who played conspicuous parts in the story of art are of but little importance except in so far as they throw light upon their style or method, or the line of art which they chose; and on the consequent direction of the progress of art under their influence. Even dates are only of importance to verify strictly the temporal relations in which the facts and the men stood to one another; and to save people from such misconceptions as calling a result the antecedent of its cause, or, inverting the order of master and disciple.

The facts which are of chief importance to a musician are the facts of the art itself; and in that respect the history of an art is fortunate, for the artistic products themselves are facts, about the existence of which there can be no manner of doubt. The inferences which they suggest may vary with different people in accordance with their artistic dispositions and preconceptions; but though the conclusions men draw about art are sometimes as disheartening as they are about every other department of human life, it is at least better to face substantial facts, on the chance of understanding them, than to build up a shadowy and unsubstantial scheme of the principles of musical development which has not even the merit of being a conscientious misconception.

The study of music itself in the light of its history and the recognition of its phases of progress and development is of more importance than all that is written about it. But it may be a valid excuse for writing about an art if it helps people to understand it better, and to enjoy it more, and more of it.

The following summary is intended as a help to the understanding of the circumstances which have made music what it is, and of the aims and efforts of the men who tried to convey their ideas by its means, and the relations in which they stood to one another; and it will not fully attain the purpose for which it is intended without reference to the actual musical facts.

The amount of music which is now easily procurable in a published form spreads over such a wide space and illustrates so copiously the various periods, from the crude experiments of early times to the wonderful achievements of recent years, that there will be little difficulty for anyone who wishes to understand the matter thoroughly to become acquainted with the works to which reference is made.

But in order to simplify the study of the actual materials it is intended to publish a second volume shortly, containing illustrations of all periods and styles of art, together with references to authorities and collections, and such particulars as may help to a fuller and more complete study of details than can easily be indicated within the limits of a primer.

SYNOPSIS.

CHAPTER I.
THE MUSIC OF THE MIDDLE AGES - - - - - - 1
Melodic Modes.—Crude notation.—Neumes.—Theorists.—Organum.—Solmisation.—Standards of Measurement of Notes.—Counterpoint.—Motets.—Early Composers.—Troubadours, Trouvères, Jongleurs, and Minnesingers.—State of Music in the thirteenth century.—Theorists again.—Music in England checked by the Wars of the Roses.—The great Netherland period from Dufay to Lasso.—The great period of pure Choral Music in Italy.—Representative early Composers of Germany.

CHAPTER II.
MUSIC IN ENGLAND FROM THE BEGINNING OF TUDOR TIMES TILL THE RESTORATION OF THE STUARTS - - - - - 10
Influence of the Tudors.—Music in the reigns of Henry VII., Henry VIII., and Elizabeth. — The transition from Roman Catholicism to Protestantism causing no break in Musical continuity in this country.—Tallys and Byrd and their followers.—Madrigals.—Coincidence of most fruitful Musical activity with period of greatest national vigour.—Music for instruments: Harpsichord, Viols, Lute, Organ.—Decline of taste for pure Choral Music.—Influence of Stuarts and Puritans.

CHAPTER III.
THE BEGINNINGS OF OPERA AND ORATORIO - - - 16
Complete Artistic revolution. — Beginning of Harmonic Music.—The ideals of the reformers.—Music-drama and Oratorio. — Monteverde. — Carissimi.— Schütz.— Opening of public Opera houses in Italian towns.—Vigour of the Operatic movement.—Cavalli.—Cesti.—Stradella.

CHAPTER IV.
THE PROGRESS OF OPERA IN VARIOUS COUNTRIES, FROM THE MIDDLE OF THE SEVENTEENTH CENTURY TILL THE TIME OF GLUCK 21
Two different branches of Operatic work, severally represented by Italy and France.—Monteverde's traditions carried on in France by Lulli.—Influence of the movement upon English Music.—The Music of the Restoration.—Purcell.—Opera in Germany.—Alessandro Scarlatti and the Neapolitan School.—The Aria.—Handel's Operatic career.—Profusion of composers of Italian Opera.

CHAPTER V.

ORATORIO IN THE TIME OF BACH AND HANDEL . - - - 30
Different lines taken by Italians and Germans.—Passion Music in Germany.—Bach's predecessors.—His Choral works.—Italian influence upon Handel.—His Oratorios.—Decline of this branch of Art for a time.

CHAPTER VI.

THE PROGRESS OF INSTRUMENTAL MUSIC UP TO THE TIME OF J. S. BACH - - - - - - - - - 36
Early instrumental Music.—In England.—In France.—Couperin.—Organ Music in Italy.—Frescobaldi.—In Germany.—The Great Italian Violinists.—Suites and Sonatas.—Handel.—J. S. Bach.—Domenico Scarlatti.

CHAPTER VII.

THE PROGRESS OF INSTRUMENTAL MUSIC IN THE EIGHTEENTH CENTURY - - - - - - - - 44
Importance of the great school of Italian violinists.—The Clavier Sonata.—In Italy.—In Germany.—Carl Philip Emmanuel Bach.—Rise of the Symphony.—Alessandro Scarlatti again.—Profusion and Crudeness of the early examples.—Development of refinement of performance.—Stamitz.—Haydn.—Mozart.—Nature of the changes effected in the latter half of the eighteenth century.—Instrumental Music branching out in all directions.—Sonatas.—Quartets, &c.

CHAPTER VIII.

OPERA IN GLUCK AND MOZART'S TIME, AND IMMEDIATELY AFTER - - - - - - 56
Reaction from the formality of Italian Opera seria.—Gluck's aims.—Piccini.—The crisis in Paris.—Difference of Mozart's position.—Italian influence.—His early Operas.—" Idomeneo " a turning-point.—German aspirations for a national Opera.—The "Singspiel."—The "Entführung aus dem Serail."—" Nozze di Figaro."—" Don Giovanni."—" Die Zauberflöte."—Lesser Opera composers.—Progress of French Grand Opera.—Spontini.

CHAPTER IX.

THE PROGRESS OF INSTRUMENTAL MUSIC TO BEETHOVEN AND HIS IMMEDIATE SUCCESSORS - - - 66
Rise of pianoforte Music.—Clementi.—Cramer.—Other prominent composers of instrumental Music.—Beethoven's early circumstances.—Predominance of Sonatas among his works.—His three periods.—His characteristics.—Enlarging principles of design.—Scherzo.—Characteristic expression.—Programme.—Hummel.—Weber.—Schubert.—Spohr.

CHAPTER X.

MODERN INSTRUMENTAL MUSIC - - - - - - - 79
Tendencies.—Berlioz.—Design.—Programme.—Instrumentation.—Mendelssohn.—Chopin.—Polish and Parisian influences.—Schumann. — Teutonic disposition. — Virtuosity.—Liszt.—Lesser representatives of instrumental Music.—Nationalities represented in instrumental Music.—One great representative of the great German school remaining.

CHAPTER XI.

MODERN OPERA - - - - - - - - - - 93
Opera in Italy since Gluck's time.—Rossini.—Other popular favourites.—Opera in France.—Light Opera.—Grand Opera.—Meyerbeer.— Gounod —Other recent French representatives.—Germany.—Aspirations after National Opera, continued.—" Fidelio."— Spohr.— Weber.—" Der Freischütz."—Weber's position and influence.—Wagner.—Early influences.—Dramatic Impulse. — Growth of powers. — Maturity first attained in "Der Ring des Nibelungen." — His aims and achievements.

CHAPTER XII.

MODERN VOCAL MUSIC - - - - - - - - 107
Solo Song.—Very characteristic of the modern phase of Music. — Schubert. — Schumann. — Brahms. — Solo Song in France.—In England.—Revival of Oratorio.—Haydn.—Spohr.—Lesser lights. — Mendelssohn. — Thriving state of Choral Music in combination with Orchestra.

CHAPTER I.

THE MUSIC OF THE MIDDLE AGES.

During the centuries in which the Roman Empire was falling to pieces, and until some of the modern states began to emerge from the chaos of barbarism and bloodshed, the development of any art was impossible. Music was only cultivated by Churchmen and was of the simplest description —confined to melody only, and indefinite in pitch and rhythm.

A certain number of scales or modes, and a few simple traditional formulas of melody, were authorised for Church use about the fourth century; and a few more modes, which were really only extensions of the earlier ones, were added some centuries later. The modes of the earlier group are always associated with the name of Ambrose, Bishop of Milan, who died 397 A.D., and are called Authentic; the later ones are associated with the name of a Pope Gregory and are called Plagal Modes. Gregory also supplemented the earlier collection of tunes by some fresh ones, and from that time forward these Church tunes were known as Cantus Planus, or Plain Chant.

The methods of writing music were extremely scanty and imperfect. The sources of the modern system of writing were the Neumes, which were marks put over the words to be sung, and indicated vaguely the inflections or changes of pitch to be used. They were made more definite as time went on by drawing coloured lines through the haphazard open order of the Neumes, which were thereby made to indicate definite relations of pitch and definite intervals; and the shapes of some of the Neumes, through which the lines were drawn, gradually changed into some of the notes which are used in modern times.

In the absence of composers, the early Middle Ages were plentifully supplied with theorists. One of the first important theoretical works of the mediæval dispensation is commonly associated with the name of Hucbald (circa 840—930 A.D.), a monk of St. Amand in Flanders. It is called Musica Enchiridiadis, and contains information about Notation, and also about the Organum or Diaphony, which was the first form of harmony, and consisted at that time chiefly of consecutive octaves, and fifths or fourths, added to the plain song of the Church.

To Guido d'Arezzo (circa 1000—1050 A.D.), another monk, is attributed the distribution of the twenty notes then used into groups of six, which were called hexachords. To him also is attributed the invention of "Solmisation," which is the naming of the notes of each hexachord by the syllables, Ut, Re, Mi, Fa, Sol, La. The origin of these syllables was a verse of a hymn to St. John, each line of which began with one of them, and each of which was sung to phrases beginning successively a note higher each time. The system of naming the notes thus has persisted into modern times; but Ut, as a bad syllable to sing, has been altered to Do, and the additional syllable Si, to complete the necessary seven notes in each octave, has been added.

In the early days there appears to have been no means of defining the relative lengths of notes; and it was not necessary to find any as long as music was purely melodic. But when men began to sing in parts some means had to be devised to keep the voices together. The first work of mark attempting to deal with this subject was by Franco of Cologne. It was called "Cantus mensurabilis," or "Measured Song," and was probably written about the middle of the twelfth century. He adopted four standards of length, and called them—(1) Maxima, or Duplex longa, (2) Longa, (3) Brevis, (4) Semibrevis. Their relations to one another varied in accordance with a time-signature which was put at the beginning of the music, which showed whether each long note was to be equal to two or to three shorter ones. In course of time the long notes dropped out of use, and the longest note now in common use, the Semibreve, is the shortest in Franco's series. He also indicated an advance in the state of harmony by expressing his preference for mixing up thirds and sixths with the so-called perfect consonances, instead of going on in rows of fifths and fourths.

This development of harmony implies the transition from diaphony to descant; as the former consisted chiefly of mere doubling of a melody or plain song at the fifth or fourth, and the latter entailed more freedom of the parts. The improvement was chiefly arrived at through the attempts of the singers to vary the monotony of the organum by the addition of ornamental notes, such as in modern times are called passing notes. These extempore attempts were imitated by composers, and hence arose the distinction of "Contrapunctus à mente," which was the extemporaneous descant of the singers, and the "Contrapunctus à pennâ," which was the written counterpoint of the regular composers.

In early days the parts were always added to the "plain chant" of the Church use, and the principle, though not the plain chant, was maintained for centuries; and even in modern times it is represented in teaching counterpoint by the practice of adding parts to a "Canto fermo."

The musicians of those days adopted also another method of singing in parts, which was to sing several tunes at once. They accommodated them by modifying the tunes a little when the roughnesses and dissonances were too conspicuous; but none of the many examples which survive sound anything but ludicrous to a modern ear. They were called Motets.

The centre of musical development in the twelfth and thirteenth centuries was Paris, which in those days was the chief focus of every kind of intellectual activity. The most distinguished musicians of the time were Léonin, Perotin, Robert de Sabillon, and Walter Odington, an Englishman.

Progress in the line of serious music was extremely slow and laborious: and the efforts of composers, for centuries, continued to be crude and barbarous; their compositions bore distinct traces of the diaphony from which their methods of part-writing were derived in the profuse successions of fifths with which they abounded. But in secular circles and among the people valuable progress was made by Troubadours, Trouvères, Jongleurs, and Minnesingers, who cultivated poetry and music under less restricted and less theoretic conditions, and with valuable results to art.

The Troubadours (from about 1087 till late in the thirteenth century) cultivated lyric poetry and the tunes which are best adapted to it. Their centre was mainly Provence and the South of France. Among them were William of Poictiers, Richard Cœur de Lion, Marcabrun, and Guiraut Riquier.

The Trouvères cultivated epic as well as lyric poetry, and also the drama. Their centre was in the Northern parts of France, and extended to the South of England. Thibaut, King of Navarre and Count of Champagne, was a noteworthy Trouvère; and so was Adam de la Hale, who wrote the play of "Robin and Marion," in which music is interspersed with dialogue. So was the English Walter Map, who wrote the story of Lancelot; and Chrestien de Troyes, who wrote its continuation; and Luc de Gast, who lived near Salisbury, and wrote the story of Tristan. The Trouvères took a very important share in the development of part-music, and cultivated the composition of secular chansons for several voices, in which a rhythmic element sometimes makes it appearance.

The Jongleurs or Menestriers (Minstrels) were the singers and storytellers of the common people, as distinguished from the courtly and aristocratic connection of the Troubadours and Trouvères. They wandered about the country, and attended fairs and markets, and had a regular guild or organisation, the centre of which was in Paris, where their headquarters continued to exist till quite modern times.

The Minnesingers occupied the same position in Germany as the Troubadours in France, and flourished later, from about 1150 A.D. till about 1260. Their most famous representatives were Heinrich der Beldecke, Walter von der Vogelweide, Wolfram von Eschenbach, who wrote the first German poem of Parsifal, and Heinrich von Meissen, sometimes called Frauenlob. The Meistersingers, who were the burgher poets and musicians of the towns, were of a later time still. Their most famous representative was Hans Sachs (1494—1576.)

In England the remains of early musical art are much scantier than in foreign countries; and the traditions are vague and unreliable. But there are distinct proofs that the country was fully up to the level of other continental nations; and one conspicuous but isolated instance, the famous Round, "Sumer is icumen in," is very far ahead of any foreign production of its time (about 1228 A.D.), both in tunefulness and management of the voice parts.

The earliest period of mediæval musical development, which culminated in the twelfth and thirteenth centuries, was succeeded by a pause in artistic progress. Various causes, social and political, disturbed the well-being of European nations, and brought back a state of distress and confusion most unfavourable to all things intellectual and artistic. The fourteenth century was barren of musical productions of any value. Such relics as the fragments of works of Guillem de Machault (1284—1369) show but little advance on the standard of the previous century. The age was more conspicuously marked by the activity of theorists, such as

De Muris (1300—1370), who wrote the "Speculum Musicæ"; Tunstede (born at Norwich, and died in Suffolk in 1369), who wrote " De musica continuâ et discretâ " in 1351 ; and De Handlo, who flourished about 1326.

The first sign of re-awakening energy was manifested in England, and its proofs are the works of John Dunstable (about 1390—1453), a composer and musician hitherto chiefly known through the appreciative allusions made to him by later writers on music—as, for instance, by the Netherlands theorist, John Tinctoris (about 1445—1511), who speaks of the "source and origin of the new art being among the English, the foremost of whom is John Dunstable." In very recent years a considerable quantity of his music has been unearthed in the Cathedral libraries of Trent, Bologna, and elsewhere, and it is clear that he was in his time regarded as the greatest composer in Europe. The style of his works is for the most part crude, but here and there passages are found which are quite intelligible and interesting to the modern ear. An English contemporary of his, who was an important representative of the art and well known in Italy as well as his own country, was John Hothby. He wrote several treatises on music, the most important of which is the " Calliopea legale." He died in 1487. Unfortunately, the good beginning made by England was nipped in the bud by causes of which the Wars of the Roses were the most conspicuous, and no sign of further musical ability can be traced in the country till the Tudor times. The equally disturbed state of France caused the centre of musical activity to pass from Paris northwards to the Netherlands, which held the pre-eminence thenceforward for a century and a half.

The first representative composer of the Netherlands period was Dufay, the dates and circumstances of whose life have only recently been traced and verified. He was a choirboy at Cambrai about 1410, a member of the Papal Choir in 1428, rose to first rank as a composer, was a long while in the service of Philip le Bon of Burgundy, and of his famous son, Charles the Bold, became a Canon of Cambrai in 1450, and died in 1474. His work is far in advance of the crude style of the earlier Parisian school, both in technique and expression, but he shows the influence of John Dunstable in sundry peculiarities of style and diction, though his work in general is more mature. He is reputed to have been the first composer who used secular tunes for Canti Fermi in the place of the old Ecclesiastical plain song—a practice which attained unfortunate notoriety in later days.

Among his most prominent fellow-composers were Faugues (born 1415), Firmin Caron (circa 1460), and his own personal friend, Binchois, who died at Lille in 1460. The most distinguished composer of the next generation was Antoine Busnois, born in 1440, in Flanders. He was in the service of Charles the Bold and died 1482. In his works is found a further progress in smoothness and equality of style, and specimens of well-managed imitation. The latter feature soon attracted composers so strongly that they began to lose sight of expression in their search after ingenuity, and expended all their powers on the contrivance of futile and mechanical canons. Of this kind of misplaced labour, Okeghem was the principal representative. He was born in Flanders early in the fifteenth century, and lived till 1513. He was looked upon as one of the greatest of European composers, and was in the service of Charles VII. and Louis XI. of France. But, notwithstanding his reputation, nearly everything to be found of his is marred by features of positive ugliness, probably owing to the misdirection of his energies. He was famous as a master however, and especially as the master of Josquin des Près (born about 1450), the greatest composer of the next generation, and among the first genuine geniuses in musical history. In Josquin's works there are many examples of the most exquisite vocal effect and passages of noble and sympathetic musical expression. He excelled alike in Church music and in secular chansons. He was one of the numerous Netherlands composers who found employment in Italy, and was in the Papal Choir from 1471 to 1484. He died at Condé in 1521. Among his pupils the most famous were Jean Mouton (died 1522) and Nicholas Gombert (born 1495). The latter carried the traditions of the school to Madrid, where he was in the service of Charles V. He was a very prolific composer, and a good one.

A composer of scarcely less gift and feeling than Josquin was Obrecht, who was Chapel Master at Utrecht when Erasmus was a choirboy there, and lived from 1430 to 1506. With him may be fitly mentioned Brumel, Compère (died 1518), and Pierre de la Rue (died 1510), who were pupils of Okeghem.

THE MUSIC OF THE MIDDLE AGES.   7

During the lives of Josquin and Obrecht the first development of the art of printing took place, which soon had great influence in the diffusion of music; and their compositions were among the first that were printed.

In the latter part of the fifteenth and throughout the sixteenth century the Netherlands and Belgium produced a large number of great musicians, most of whom found employment in Italy. Among these Adrian Willaert (1480—1562) was famous for the choral works for a double choir which he wrote for use at the Cathedral of St. Mark's at Venice, where he was Maëstro di Capella; also for his madrigals, from which he won the reputation of being the first madrigal writer. Contemporary with him, and also attached to St. Mark's, was Philip Verdelot (about 1500—1567), who was early in the field as a composer of madrigals, canzonas, and other works of the kind. He also had some claim to be considered the first of the madrigal writers, as a number of his were published in a collection which came out at Venice in 1533. Jacques Arcadelt (about 1495—1560) was also famous for his madrigals, of which he published several sets in Venice, beginning in the year 1538, which met with great favour.

The first Italian to come prominently before the world was Constanzo Festa (about 1490—1545). Madrigals of his were included in the same early collection with Verdelot's, and also in Arcadelt's. His advent marked the beginning of the time when the pre-eminence in music passed from the Netherlands to Italy. Netherlands composers of great power still came before the world, such as Jacques Clement, commonly known as Clemens non Papa, who died about 1558; Cyprian van Rore (1516—1565), who succeeded Willaert at St. Mark's; Waelrent (circa 1518—1595); Philippus del Monte (circa 1521—1600), and the famous Orlando di Lasso (1532—1594); but the Italians rapidly surpassed them, and before the end of the century had wrested the supremacy from them. Lasso's reputation overtopped that of all his countrymen. He was a man of interesting personal character, and a lover of strange experiments in music. The most famous amongst his very numerous works is his setting of seven Penitential Psalms, which contains some of the most curious effects ever contrived for unaccompanied voices, and a great deal that is both characteristic and beautiful.

The spread of Italian musical gift was as rapid as its rise;

and before the end of the century Venice produced Zarlino (1519—1590) the theorist, and the two Gabrielis, Andrea (1510—1586) and Giovanni (1557—1613), great masters of choral art and experimenters in instrumental music; while from other parts of Italy came Claudio Merulo (1533—1604), the famous organist; Marenzio (1550—1599), the greatest of the madrigal writers, and Pierluigi Sante da Palestrina, the greatest master of the old pure choral style, in whom the progress of the previous centuries came to a final climax. Palestrina was born at the town from which he takes his name, about 1528. He went early to Rome and studied music under Claude Goudimel, a Frenchman who afterwards became a Calvinist, and set the French version of the Psalms by Marot and Beza, and perished in the massacre of St. Bartholomew in 1572. The most famous of Palestrina's works is the Mass known as "Missa Papæ Marcelli," which is commonly said to have been written in 1565 at the desire of the Commission appointed by Pope Pius IV. to enquire into the abuses and anomalies which had almost overwhelmed Church music. It certainly produced a great impression at the time it first came before the world, but several circumstances combine to make the well known story doubtful. The amount of his musical compositions is very large indeed; consisting of masses, hymns, motets, lamentations, madrigals, &c., all for voices unaccompanied. His style is characterised by a quiet nobility and dignity of expression, which make it the most perfect and serenely beautiful religious music ever written; while his extraordinary instinct for choral effect of the purest kind enabled him to produce exquisite and subtle effects of sound with the voices, which in that particular style have never been surpassed. He died in 1594, and his death marked the turning point to the decadence of the old choral style, and the beginning of a new epoch in art; of which the first experimenters in opera and oratorio were the earliest representatives. Among his contemporaries who are worthy of being honourably remembered are Morales the Spaniard, who entered the Papal Choir about 1540; and Nanini (1545—1607), both of whom are said to have been fellow-pupils with him under Goudimel. Another Spaniard, Vittoria, a little younger than Palestrina, was a very great master of choral art, and so was Giovanni Croce (1559—1609). Orazio Vecchi (1551—1605), Anerio (1560—1630), and Allegri (1586—1662) were also very important

Italian representatives of the latest phase of the pure choral style.

As sometimes happens in human affairs, the nation that was destined to go farthest was slow to develop. In these early times Germany was not so liberally represented by great composers as some other nations. But the country had produced a few very remarkable representatives of the art, of whom the most notable was Henrich Isaak, who lived in the fifteenth century, contemporary with Busnois and Okeghem. He produced a large quantity of fine church music, and some secular songs, among which was one that in later times became one of the most famous of chorales. Johann Walther (1496—1570), the friend of Luther, took an important share in starting the music of the Reformed Church, and brought out the first Protestant Hymn Book in 1524. Soon after followed Ludwig Senfl, Jacob Händl, commonly known by his Latinised name of Gallus; Antonius Scandellus, Thomas Stolzer, and Paulus Hofheimer. The latest important representative of the early form of choral art in Germany was Hans Leo Hassler (circa 1564—1612), who was a pupil of Andrea Gabrieli in Venice.

CHAPTER II.

MUSIC IN ENGLAND FROM THE BEGINNING OF TUDOR TIMES TILL THE RESTORATION OF THE STUARTS.

WHEN the Wars of the Roses came to an end in 1485, and the astute government of Henry VII. gave England time to regain her balance, Music began to be cultivated to some purpose in this country. The Tudors appear to have been a genuinely musical family, and their influence upon all kinds of arts was uniformly good. Henry VII. himself had a large musical establishment, and the taste and skill of his son, afterwards Henry VIII., were favourable to the state of music at Court. The standard of musical composition in this reign was not very high, but excellent purpose is shown in the works of Dr. Robert Fayrfax, Sheryngham, Turges, Newark, Phelyppes, and others.

In Henry VIII.'s reign these somewhat tentative beginnings passed into vigorous exercise of musical faculty. The King himself produced some excellent compositions, and set a good example by his ability in singing at sight, which accomplishment came before long to be considered a necessary part of the equipment of a properly educated gentleman.

Various fortunate circumstances caused the transition from Roman Catholicism to Protestantism in England to be gradual and moderate, with the happy result that the noble style of the Roman Church music of that age passed without change into the music of the Reformed Church. Before the Reformation became an accomplished fact, there were already a number of composers and musicians of great ability in the country, most of whom gave the Reformed Church the benefit of their powers, sometimes without forsaking the old Church themselves.

Of those who came earliest into the field at this time, the most noteworthy are John Taverner (organist of Christ Church, Oxford, about 1530), John Redford (1491—1547), Robert Johnson, John Sheppard (organist of Magdalen at Oxford, 1542), Robert White (organist of Ely, 1562—1567; died 1575), and Christopher Tye (organist of Ely, 1541; died 1572). The last-named held a most prominent position among musicians, and did great service to the cause of the art of the Reformed Church by the dignified and masculine style of his compositions. He was appointed Music Master to Edward VI., in whose reign the movement towards Protestantism, under Archbishop Cranmer's guidance, became more rapid and decisive.

When the English Service Book was compiled in 1550, the traditional plain song used in the old Church was adapted to it by John Merbecke, thereby confirming the musical identity of the old and new services.

In the new generation of composers, Thomas Tallys (born soon after 1510, died 1585) occupied a foremost place. He wrote works for both Roman and Protestant use which are solid and masterly, and have a distinct character of their own. His pupil, William Byrd (born about 1538, died 1623), had still more comprehensive talents, as he wrote admirable madrigals and instrumental music for keyed instruments, as well as Church music of the finest and noblest quality. Both Tallys and Byrd maintained their sympathy with the old Church till the end of their days, and the character of the music written for both the new and the old ritual is so similar as often to be indistinguishable; indeed many of the works used in the English service as anthems were merely adaptations from motets and *Cantiones sacræ*, or similar compositions, with the words translated from the original Latin into the more familiar English tongue.

In Elizabeth's reign the progress of the previous years came to a brilliant climax. Tallys and Byrd by her time were men of mature years, and were followed by a younger generation fully worthy of the traditions they had established. Music has never been held in greater honour, nor cultivated with more judgment and high artistic sense, than at the time when the vigour of the nation in enterprise, adventure, and war was at its highest. The memorable year 1588, in which the huge Spanish Armada, with its 130 ships and 29,000 men, was defeated and dispersed, is marked in musical history by the definite beginning of the English Madrigal period. A few isolated examples had made their appearance previously, such as the madrigal "In going to my lonely bed," attributed to Edwards (1523—1566), and some secular part-music published by Thomas Whythorne; but the publication of the first series of the Musica Transalpina, by Nicholas Yonge, in this year, is the decisive beginning of a series of publications of madrigals and similar works which followed in rapid succession for a quarter of a century. This work was a collection of the finest madrigals, chiefly by Italian composers of the time, and the editor, Yonge, appended a preface which comments on the growing taste for part-singing and the general appreciation of madrigals among cultivated musical amateurs. His venture and his views were thoroughly justified by what followed. The first new composer who made his appearance in the field was Thomas Morley, who excelled in all the known forms of Art, whether in Church music or in madrigals, or in the charming ballets in which he combined the subtleties of the madrigal style with the brightness and freshness of the Italian balletti. His first publication was a collection of canzonets, which came out in 1593. In 1594 followed a set of madrigals, and in 1595 the first set of his ballets. In 1597 he published his "Introduction to Practical Music," which contains invaluable information about the state of music in his time. In the same year that admirable master, Thomas Weelkes, made his first appearance in print with a set of fine madrigals; and in the same year also appeared the first set of the beautiful "Songs or Ayres of Four Parts," by John Dowland (1562—1626), which mark, by their simple character and the definiteness of their form, the approach of the new era in music; a characteristic which may have come about through the fact that Dowland was a great lute player. In the next year, 1598, appeared the first set of madrigals by the greatest of English madrigal writers, John Wilbye; in which we find the richest development of the madrigal form combined with wit, vigour, and poetic feeling. The next year saw the appearance of ballets and madrigals by Thomas Weelkes and others, and the year 1599 the appearance of madrigals by John Benet, one of the most versatile and expressive of composers in this line. In 1601 appeared a superb monument of the skill and artistic sense of the musicians of Elizabeth's reign in the "Triumphs of Oriana," which was a collection of twenty-five madrigals by English composers, made in honour of the Queen; almost all of which have distinct merit, while some are of the highest order. Of those composers who appeared first after this time the most important were Thomas Bateson, whose set came out in 1604; Michael Este, also 1604; and Orlando Gibbons (born at Cambridge, 1583, died at Canterbury, 1625), whose set came out in 1612—that is, nine years after the death of Elizabeth. The energy generated in Elizabeth's days lasted on into the days of the Stuarts, and the last-named writer was the greatest and most comprehensive composer of all the school, excelling even more in his superb music for the Church than in his fine madrigals. Of all the Church music of this period indeed, Gibbons's is the highest type, and marks the culmination of the genuinely English branch of the polyphonic school, which had come to its culmination in Italy at an earlier date in the works of Palestrina.

The survey of the music of the Elizabethan period would not be complete without reference to the work of a few composers who devoted their energies almost exclusively to Church music, such as Richard Farrant (circa 1530—1580), Elway Bevin, who published a "Shorte Introduction to the Art of Musicke" in 1631; and Adrian Batten (circa 1590—1640).

Reference is also due to the very serviceable work done in the line of instrumental music in the pieces written for "Virginals," by a considerable number of composers, the most ingenious of which, from a technical point of view, were written by John Bull (circa 1563—1628)—an organist of universal fame—and the most interesting by Orlando Gibbons. Many collections of virginal music were made about this time. The most famous is the MS. known as Queen Elizabeth's Virginal Book, containing over 400 pieces, mainly by English composers. It could not, however, have belonged to Queen Elizabeth, as several of the pieces in it were certainly written after her death. Another collection is "Lady Nevill's Book," of forty-two pieces, all by Byrd. W. Forster's Virginal Book, dated 1624, contains seventy-eight pieces, and Benjamin Cosyn's, ninety-eight. The first printed book of such music was the Parthenia, which came out in 1611, and contained a number of pieces by Byrd, Bull, and Gibbons—some of those by the latter composer being specially fine. The pieces in all these collections consist mainly of old dances, such as pavanas and galliards, and preludes, fantasias, and arrangements of choral works. They indicate a considerable taste for such music and no little development of technique.

This country was indeed brilliantly represented in every department of art then known. Music for sets of viols of as good quality as any in Europe was produced by such composers as Thomas Morley, Michael Este, Alfonso Ferrabosco (circa 1580—1652), and Orlando Gibbons. Lute music was represented by John Dowland, who was lute player to Christian IV. of Denmark. Organ music was represented by John Bull and Peter Philipps. The latter lived abroad most of his life, chiefly in Flanders. He was one of the foremost representatives of organ music of the day, and a notable musician in every respect. He produced admirable madrigals, motets, and other choral music, besides organ music.

During the unfortunate rule of the Stuarts the standard of music rapidly declined. But though Stuart taste had considerable influence upon the direction taken by music, especially in the case of the second Charles, the lowering of the standard of choral music cannot fairly be laid to their charge any more than to the Puritans. Musical historians are fond of holding the fanaticism of the latter answerable for the extinction of choral music; and no doubt they put the finishing blow to a crumbling edifice. But the decadence began long before the Civil War broke out. The last great representative of the choral epoch in Europe died in the very week Charles married Henrietta Maria. And though the complete change which had come upon music about the year 1600 was slower in influencing the art in England than in other countries, it was bound to bring the great era of pure choral art to an end there as elsewhere, without the assistance of either Stuarts or Puritans. But it is noteworthy that though the cultivation of the choral style came to an end, the wave of musical enthusiasm and ability did not by any means cease abruptly. It was deflected, as in other countries, into new channels; and England continued to be ahead of all the countries of Europe in the new lines of art, such as instrumental music and theatrical music, till the death of Purcell. Lute music was brilliantly represented by Thomas Mace, who brought out his famous book, "Musick's Monument," in 1676. Christopher Sympson carried the art of viol playing to the highest pitch then known, and brought out his most important book, "The Division Violist, or an Introduction to the Playing on a Ground," in 1659, the year after Cromwell died. Music for sets of viols was represented by the Fancies and sets of "Ayres" and other pieces by John Jenkins (1592—1678), William Lawes (born about 1590, killed at siege of Chester, 1645), Matthew Locke (born early in the seventeenth century, and died 1689), Thomas Tomkins (circa 1590—1656), and many others; while the new style of incidental Music to Masques and stage plays was written with much success by Henry Lawes (1595—1662), Matthew Locke, Simon Ives (died 1662), and others. In these secular directions the short period of civil war did not have any great effect upon music. Many musicians who had been active before it began undoubtedly carried on their artistic work while it was going on, and came forward with undiminished lustre after the Restoration. The wave of musical enthusiasm and ability which began in the Tudor times may therefore fairly be considered to have lasted on almost till the time when Handel came to England. For though the line of music to which composers gave their minds was changed, and Church and choral music practically fell from a grand and mature style to an almost infantile stage of experimental crudity, an equal standard of ability, comparable to the very best in other countries, was still displayed in instrumental music, solo music, and music for the stage. Before proceeding to the last stage of this period of English musical energy, the state of music in other countries must be considered.

CHAPTER III.

THE BEGINNINGS OF OPERA AND ORATORIO.

THE last quarter of the sixteenth century witnessed the culmination of pure choral music in the works of Palestrina, Lasso, Marenzio, and their fellows. It also witnessed the beginnings of a new movement, which amounted to no less than a complete artistic revolution.

About this time a certain group of artistic and musical enthusiasts entered into speculations on the possibility of developing a new kind of musical art, in the form of solo music with instrumental accompaniment. Their central idea was to revive the style of performance of the ancient Greek dramas; and in connection with this they made experiments in the musical declamation of sonnets and poems of various kinds.

The most prominent of those who took part in the earliest stages of the movement were Vincenzio Galilei, the father of the famous philosopher and physicist; Emilio del Cavaliere, a composer; Rinuccini, a poet; Giulio Caccini, a singer and composer; Jacopo Peri, a musical amateur of ability and taste; and Giovanni Bardi, Count of Vernio, in whose house at Florence they used frequently to meet. The first recorded examples of their experiments were three Pastorals by Cavaliere, called "Il Satiro" (1590), "La disperazione di Fileno" (1590), and "Il giuoco della cieca" (1595). These were looked upon as containing the first successful examples of recitative, with the invention of which Cavaliere is accordingly sometimes credited. They were followed by the drama "Dafne," which was written by Rinuccini and set by Peri in 1597.

These early experiments have unfortunately been lost; the first example of their reforming energy which has survived is the "Euridice," which was written by Rinuccini and set by Peri, and performed on the occasion of the marriage of Henry IV. of France and Maria de' Medici in Florence, in 1600. This work is of a very slender description, consisting mainly of formless recitatives interspersed with short passages of instrumental music called "Ritornelli," and equally short and unimportant choruses. The object of the composer appears to have been mainly to declaim the poem without attempting striking musical effects, and to look to the drama to supply the interest. Caccini also set the poem of "Euridice," and wrote a book on the new movement, called the "Nuove Musiche."

In the same year (1600) Cavaliere's Oratorio "La Rappresentazione di Anima e di Corpo" was first performed in Rome, shortly after the death of the composer. The work was a product of the same order of ideas which gave birth to the first music-dramas; but its immediate antecedents were different. It appears to have been suggested by the performances which had been given in the Oratory of Santa Maria in Vallicella at Rome, of plays founded on Biblical subjects and combined with simple music. These had been instituted by Philippo Neri, the founder of the Congregation of the Oratorians, for religious purposes; and it appears that Cavaliere's Oratorio had also a religious purpose, and that the familiar name which has become universal was derived from the place where these earlier works had been performed. The name "Oratorio," however, did not come into use till considerably later. The first to use it in a published work is said to have been Francesco Balducci, who died 1642. The earlier examples were sometimes described as "Dramma sacra per Musica." In style Cavaliere's work appears to be finer than Peri's, as the prologue is a noble specimen of the early kind of declamation. The choruses are simple, like the "Laudi spirituali," or hymns which had been introduced in Philippo Neri's plays. The new movement was carried on by a good many energetic composers in the same line, and several more sacred musical dramas were produced in the early part of this century, as, for instance, "The lament of the Virgin Mary," by Capollini, 1627; Mazzocchi's "Martyrdom of St. Abbundio," &c., 1631; "St. Alessio," by Laudi, 1634; and others.

The most important work of the time was done in the line of the secular music-drama, which made great strides in the hands of Claudio Monteverde. This remarkable composer (born 1568) began his career as a violist in the Duke of Mantua's band, and afterwards served him as Maëstro di Capella until the time that he was advanced to the more important post of Maëstro at St. Mark's at Venice. His genius was of the revolutionary and experimental order; and the limitations and refinements of the old choral music were little to his taste. Even in his works for voices alone he endeavoured to obtain dramatic and theatrical effects, and used more harsh and striking chords than had been usual in choral music. His success in this line was much less marked than in his works for the theatre. The two first of these, "Arianna" and "Orfeo," which appeared in 1607, at once made him the most prominent of living composers. The former is lost, all but a fragment—the latter has survived complete, and gives a clear indication of the direction in which the art was moving. Monteverde in this shows daring and force in the treatment of his subject. He uses a large group of instruments for his accompaniments and ritornelli, with a certain crude sense of effect. As in the works of Peri and Caccini, there is a very large quantity of formless recitative, and very little that is constructively definite; but he evidently endeavoured to intensify the dramatic situations by the character of the music, and to follow the varying shades of feeling expressed in the dialogue by characteristic intervals and harmonies. He also had a considerable instinct for histrionic musical effect, and worked rather for stage purposes than for purely musical effect. These early operas of his were written for special occasions, such as the marriage of the Duke of Mantua's eldest son; but he lived long enough to witness the opening of public opera-houses in Venice by Manelli and Ferrari (1637), and wrote his two last operas, "L'Adone" (1640) and "L'Incoronazione di Poppea" (1642), for them. He died in 1643. His singular pre-eminence has put the works of his contemporaries into the shade. But the "Dafne" of Gagliano, which was first performed in Mantua, and published in Florence in 1608, deserves to be remembered as representing a higher artistic conception of the form of art than the earliest examples.

The line of Oratorio was worthily carried on by Giacomo Carissimi, a composer of powers in some ways equal to Monteverde's, and gifted with more artistic judgment and reserve. He was the first master of the new school who brought the experience of a thorough training in the old artistic methods to bear upon the new forms of art; and his Oratorios, such as "Judicium Salomonis," "Jephte," "Jonas," and "Baltazar," contain really fine choruses, as well as most expressive and well written solos, and many features which show a considerable sense of dramatic effect. He also wrote several secular cantatas for solo voice, and motets and other Church music for unaccompanied choir. He lived till 1674.

THE BEGINNINGS OF OPERA AND ORATORIO. 19

In his time the budding German school was brought into contact with the new Italian movement through Heinrich Schütz (1585—1672), who came from Saxony to study under Giovanni Gabrieli (1557—1612), at St. Mark's in Venice, early in the eighteenth century. He here came into contact with the theories of the new school as well as with Gabrieli's own original experiments in direct musical expression by choral and instrumental means; and when he went back to Germany he gave characteristic evidence of his Teutonic love of the mystic and pathetic as well as of his Italian training in his Oratorio "The Resurrection" (1623), and in his noteworthy settings of the "Passion" according to the four Evangelists, and in various Psalms. He also set a German translation of Rinuccini's drama of "Dafne," which had served Peri as a libretto in the earliest years of the new movement.

The earliest composers of mark who profited largely by the opening of public opera-houses were Monteverde's pupil, P. F. Cavalli (1599—1676), and Carissimi's pupil, Antonio Cesti (circa 1620—1669). They both show the influence of their masters, as the former had the greatest instinct for stage effect and the latter the more genuine musical instinct.

Cavalli wrote an enormous number of operas. At least twenty-six are still preserved in the library of St. Mark at Venice. The most famous was "Giasone" (1649), which contains a few strong points of dramatic effect and some characteristic and clear passages of declamation, but does not show much advance in treatment of instruments or design upon the works of Monteverde. His fame spread to foreign countries, and he was summoned to Paris, in 1660 and 1662, to superintend the performance of his "Xerse" and "Ercole amante" for certain court festivities.

Cesti practically represents a later generation, for though he was busy with opera writing at the same time as Cavalli, his general standard of art shows a decided advance in all departments. His treatment of instruments is much freer and more effective; his general style of writing is more mature; while his sense of tune and construction is so good that it justifies his being considered the best melodist of the middle of the seventeenth century. Among many excellent operas his best was "Orontea," which was brought out in 1649 in Venice, for the opening of one of the new theatres, and maintained a vigorous popularity for thirty years. "La Dori" (1663) and "La Magnanimita d'Alessandro" also contain excellent music. He also wrote many cantatas for solo voices, which contain charmingly melodious arias.

A noteworthy contemporary of these composers was Legrenzi (born about 1625), who was Maëstro di Capella at St. Mark's in Venice from 1685 to 1690, where he did good service by re-organising the instrumental forces into something resembling the scheme of modern orchestras, and wrote a number of good operas.

One of the most interesting figures in the musical history of the century was Alessandro Stradella. He also was a pupil of Carissimi's, and his powers excited the imagination of his contemporaries to such an extent that he became the hero of one of the most remarkable romances in musical history. He was undoubtedly a composer of great powers, which are shown in his Oratorio "San Giovanni Baptista," by very free treatment of instruments, well and clearly designed arias, fine and broad choruses, and a considerable power of dramatic expression. His work shows the artistic thoroughness of the Carissimi school, combining respect for the old choral traditions with mastery of the new artistic theories. His work is more mature than that of any other composer of the century before Alessandro Scarlatti, and is sometimes fully on a level with that notable master, and rather suggestive both of his style and Handel's.

CHAPTER IV.

THE PROGRESS OF OPERA IN VARIOUS COUNTRIES, FROM THE MIDDLE OF THE SEVENTEENTH CENTURY TILL THE TIME OF GLUCK.

THE new movement, which gave birth to modern Opera and Oratorio about 1600 A.D., soon branched out into two distinct lines, which have maintained their characteristics till the present day. The first prominent representatives of these were Monteverde and Carissimi. The former stands at the head of the modern composers who study effect more than art; the latter at the head of those who study art more than effect. Monteverde ostentatiously rejected the traditions of his predecessors, to leave himself free to carry out his dramatic ideals. Carissimi endeavoured to make use of the accumulated wisdom of earlier generations to guide him to the fittest artistic expression of his musical ideas.

The traditions of Monteverde were handed on to his pupil Cavalli (1599-1676), who became the foremost operatic composer of his time; and by him they were introduced into France, whither his great reputation had penetrated. But the characteristics of French opera were different from the ideals of the Italians, being founded mainly on ballet and spectacular display. The Italians in those days cared little for ballet; and to make Cavalli's operas palatable to French audiences, ballet airs had to be supplied. The task fell to the lot of Jean Baptiste Lulli, a young man who had been sent from Italy to the French Court and had ingratiated himself with King Louis XIV., by his talent for supplying dance music for the "Mascarades," in which the King and his Court took pleasure in dancing. Lulli was by this means brought into direct contact with Cavalli's works, and the experience stood him in good stead when he came to write operas some ten years later. In the meanwhile he kept in touch with the stage by writing incidental music to several of Molière's "Comédies Ballets," in which he himself sometimes acted; and by composing "divertissements dansés," in which line he had made considerable success as early as 1658 with "Alcidiane."

The foremost French composer of the time was Robert Cambert (1628-1677), who is sometimes described as the first composer of French opera. He made his first appearance with noteworthy success in a work called "La Pastorale," in 1659, which is described in the language of the time as "the first French comedy in music." It was followed by "Ariane" in 1661. In 1669 Louis founded the "Académie Royale de Musique" for the performance of operas and gave the management into the hands of Perrin, who, being a kind of poet, provided the librettos and associated Cambert with himself as composer; and they produced "Pomona" with success in 1671.

Lulli, however, had the ear of the King, and persuaded him to abrogate Perrin's rights and hand them over to him; giving him sole power for the performance of opera in Paris. Cambert, by this means, was driven out of France and took refuge at the Court of Charles II., where he remained till his death in 1677.

Lulli then began his important operatic career with the *pasticcio*, "Les fêtes de l'Amour et de Bacchus" in 1672, and followed it up with his first complete opera, "Cadmus," in 1673. From that time till his death, in 1687, he continued to supply operas year after year; the most noteworthy being "Alceste" (1674), "Thésée" (1675), "Atys" (1676), "Bellérophon" (1679), "Persée" (1682), "Phaëton" (1683), "Amadis" (1684), "Roland" (1685), and "Armida" (1686). The last was "Acis and Galatea" (1686). The scheme of his operas was well contrived for spectacular effect, apparently on the same plan as that adopted in Cambert's works. The plays were interspersed with ballets and choruses, and scenes in which a number of persons were effectively grouped on the stage; and the development of each act shows considerable power of artistic management and insight for stage effect, which are made the more available by the allegorical character of the subjects. The best features of the works are the overtures, which are solid and dignified, and the many fine passages of declamatory music, which comprise some high dramatic qualities of expression. Lulli's work is immensely superior to Cavalli's in technical mastery of resource; its drawbacks are the heaviness and monotony of his instrumental accompaniments, and his carelessness of artistic finish. He had no rivals in France, and left no one capable of immediately carrying on the development of French opera. But he set his seal upon the form of art, and French opera has maintained its distinctive features ever since. He had a very keen eye for business, and left a fortune of 800,000 livres behind him when he died in 1687.

The influence of the French style became powerful in England when Charles II. was recalled to the throne in 1660. He brought with him from foreign countries an enthusiasm for it, and when he restored the establishments of the Chapels Royal he endeavoured to replace the grand old style of Tallis and Byrd and Gibbons, for which he had no taste, by the music of viols, and solos, and things generally of a livelier cast, like French music.

Most of the singing men and organists and composers of the old *régime*, such as Captain Cook and Christopher Gibbons and W. Child, were not sufficiently in touch with the new movement to supply him with what he wanted. So he took advantage of a manifestation of great talent among some of the choirboys of the Chapel Royal to send one of the most gifted of them, Pelham Humfrey (born 1645), to France to learn his business there. After a year or so this boy came back thoroughly imbued with the French style, and became a fit leader to the younger generation of composers, represented by John Blow (1648—1708) and Michael Wise (born about 1648, died 1687), who were among the choirboys of the same standing as himself. Unfortunately Humfrey himself only survived to the age of twenty-seven, and made no more than a beginning, with some singular and sometimes interesting experiments in Church music. But among the choirboys of the next generation appeared the remarkable genius, Henry Purcell (1658—1695), whose nature readily absorbed the influences of the new movement, both in its French and Italian aspects, and in the short space of the thirty-seven years of his life produced an enormous quantity of music of every kind, both instrumental and vocal, comprising operas, songs, sonatas for strings, suites, and church music.

England had already at this time a distinct type of stage piece associated with music, which became the model of the occasional early experiments in opera. A kind of entertainment called a Masque had been popular at Court for many generations. All the Stuarts were fond of theatrical performances, and in Charles I.'s reign the Court constantly entertained itself with such masques, in which the Queen and her ladies and little Prince Charles took part. The words of these works were written by the most distinguished poets, and the music by the ablest musicians attainable, while the scenery was managed by the famous architect, Inigo Jones. These occurred annually almost up to the date of the outbreak of civil war. Among their characteristics is a certain literary flavour, and a preponderance of fanciful elements over dramatic; and these qualities re-appeared in the operatic experiments which were made after the Restoration.

Purcell began his connection with the theatre by writing excellent incidental music and dance tunes for a number of plays—such as "Epsom Wells," "Aurenge Zebe," and "The Libertine," in 1676; "Abdelazor," 1677; "Timon of Athens," 1678; "The Virtuous Wife," 1680, and so on. His first opportunity on a sufficiently extensive scale to be called an opera was the setting of a work called "Dido and Æneas," by Nahum Tate, which he made in 1680. For the time when this was written it is marvellously rich in expression, definite in character, and very interesting in harmony. It evidently made an impression upon the musical people of the day; but it was the last opportunity Purcell had of writing for the stage for a long while. In 1680 he was appointed organist of Westminster Abbey, and thenceforward he devoted all his abilities for some years to Church music, of which he produced an enormous quantity, of characteristic but very unequal quality. It was not till after the accession of William III. (1688) that he had another opportunity of writing the music for an opera. The first of his remaining works in this line was "Dioclesian," which was produced in 1690. His principal work of the kind was "King Arthur," which came out in 1691. The poem was written by Dryden, and had the literary qualities to be expected of him. Purcell's music was practically incidental, though there is a great deal of it, comprising many characteristic choruses, and solos, and songs, and excellent dance music of a very solid kind. In later years he produced a great deal more incidental music, and dances and songs to various plays, such as "The Fairy Queen" (1692), "The Indian Queen" (1692), two parts of "Don Quixote" (1694 and 1695), and "Bonduca" (1695).

Purcell died in 1695, and left the country without any composer of sufficient powers to carry on the work he had so well begun, till the advent of Handel in 1710 put a new aspect on affairs. Purcell's style is very individual, and his genius is of a high order; but the immature state of music at the time when he lived, as well as the absence of good models in the new style of art, militate against the general equality of his work, and prevent his holding as high a position in public favour as his genius deserves.

Germany shared the same fate as England at this time, as far as the establishment of any characteristically national opera was concerned. For though many composers took in hand the form of art known as the Singspiel, and though Reinhard Keiser (1673—1739) produced no less than 116 operas, mostly for his Theatre in Hamburg, no one was able to maintain a characteristically German quality of work, and in the next generation opera in Germany fell under the spell of the Italian style.

In Italy the highest position among opera composers at this time was held by the great Alessandro Scarlatti (1659—1725). He was a pupil of Carissimi, and carried on the artistic traditions of the line of art he represented.

His first opera, "L' Onesta nell' Amore," came out in Rome in 1680. But most of his works were written for Naples, and with him began the great days of the Neapolitan school, whose composers were celebrated for the excellence of their writing for the voice.

In the course of his career Scarlatti produced over 100 operas, most of which have been lost. Those that remain show great advance on the work of his predecessors in maturity of technical workmanship and style. The instruments are much more effectively and freely used, the arias are better balanced and better developed, and his fund of melody is richer and more varied. He also did his art signal service by frequently adopting a form of instrumental overture in three or four movements, which was the ultimate source of the modern orchestral symphony.

The drawback of his type of opera is the constant and wearisome alternation of recitatives and arias, which latter are always in the same form, with a leading portion and a contrasting portion, and a "Da capo," or simple repetition of the first portion to conclude with. Scarlatti was doubtless not the inventor of the form, but he used it with monotonous persistence, to the detriment of his works as wholes.

He was the last Italian of the early period who occupied the foremost place in the world as an operatic composer. In succeeding generations the German composers learnt their art in the school of the Italians, and for some time maintained pre-eminence as writers of Italian opera.

The first to wrench the sceptre from the hands of the Italians was G. F. Handel (1685—1759), who began his career as a subordinate violin player in the band of Keiser's Opera House in Hamburg. From the position of violinist he was promoted to that of cembalist or accompanist on the harpsichord, and in Keiser's Theatre he produced his two first operas, "Almira" (1705) and "Nero" (1706); and here he formed the acquaintance of the able and energetic Johann Matheson (1681—1764), who was one of his first friends and advisers. About the year 1707 he succeeded in carrying out his long-cherished project of going to Italy; and he there produced "Rodrigo" in Florence in 1707 and "Agrippina" in Venice in 1708. He soon learnt all the arts of the Italians, and surpassed them in their own lines; and this experience had the profoundest influence on his style and his career.

In 1710 he came to England, which was sorely in need of a man of sufficiently comprehensive powers to supply the fashionable world with operatic performances. He was invited to produce an opera, and wrote "Rinaldo" in a fortnight; which is not only one of the quickest pieces of work ever done by a musician, but one of his best operas. It came out in 1711, and was enthusiastically received, and his position in England was instantly assured.

But he did not at first devote much of his time to opera, as he had to attend to his duties as Capellmeister to the Elector of Hanover (afterwards George I.), and to his duties as Capellmeister to the Duke of Chandos at Cannons. For the latter he wrote the first version of "Esther" (under the name of "Haman and Mordecai," a masque), and "Acis and Galatea," and the "Chandos Anthems." His mind was concentrated more decisively on opera work from the year 1720, when the Royal Academy of Music—for the performance of operas—was founded by various people connected with the Court. The enterprise was opened with Handel's "Radamisto," which was a phenomenal success. Buononcini and Ariosti were also engaged as composers, and some of the greatest living singers, such as Cuzzoni, Faustina Bordoni, and Senesino were engaged to sing. Unluckily, a series of misfortunes brought the establishment to an untimely end. The violent rivalries of Cuzzoni and Faustina and their followers threw the Opera House into confusion, and the counter attractions of the famous "Beggar's Opera" at the Theatre in Lincoln's Inn Fields (1728) reduced the numbers of the audience, and the Royal Academy of Music finally collapsed with a loss of £50,000. For this institution Handel wrote fourteen operas, many among his best works of the kind, such as "Radamisto" (1720), "Ottone" (1722), "Giulio Cesare" (1723), "Tamerlane" (1724), "Rodelinda" (1725), "Scipione" (1726), "Alessandro" (1726), "Tolomeo" (1728).

Being undismayed by disaster, and confident of his own abilities, he determined to run an Opera House on his own account, and entered into partnership with one Heidegger for the purpose. Unfortunately the good will with which he had been regarded by the people at Court turned to deadly enmity, possibly through the machinations of the Italian composer Buononcini, who started a rival house with the assistance of some members of the aristocracy in 1733. A bitter war was carried on till 1737, when the aristocracy's opera house collapsed, and Handel only managed to hold on for a fortnight longer. The tide had turned so fiercely against him that one new opera after another was a failure, he lost his savings, and his health gave way. But a short visit to Germany revived him and he returned to the charge by writing a few more operas for a fresh venture under Heidegger. His last was "Deidamia," produced in 1740, when he was fifty-four years old.

The period of his Oratorio work slightly overlaps the operatic time. "Esther," "Deborah," "Saul," and "Israel in Egypt" all made their appearance before 1740. But the greater part of the works by which he is best known were produced after the long effort of his operatic career was over.

His operatic works form the climax of the first stage in the history of opera. In plan they are much the same as Scarlatti's; and though his arias are characterised by a greater wealth of melody and a greater resource of treatment and expression, the same monotonous alternation of recitative and aria ruins the effect of the works as wholes. The materials in detail are often superb; and though he played into the hands of the singers, who were already beginning to feel and show their power, he did not fall into the degree of empty conventional insincerity which characterised the works of the writers of Italian opera in the next generation. His position was that of a caterer for the public, but the quality of what he gave them was intrinsically worthy of his great powers.

Meanwhile the popularity of opera in Italy evoked a perfect flood of fairly artistic works by a great variety of composers, all of whom had more feeling for suitable writing for solo singers than for dramatic effect. The influence of the Neapolitan school, of which Alessandro Scarlatti was the greatest representative and progenitor, became enormous. Most of the leading composers were either pupils of his or pupils of his pupils—such as Gaetano Greco—or pupils of his successor, Durante (1693—1755). Among those were Leonardo Leo (1694—1746), a composer of really solid and notable powers; Leonardo Vinci (born 1690, poisoned 1732); Nicolo Porpora (1686—1766); David Perez (1711—1778); Nicolo Jomelli (1714—1774); Domenico Scarlatti, Alessandro's son, and famous as a player on and writer for the harpsichord (1683—1757); the writer of native Neapolitan buffo opera, Logroscino (1700—1763); and the short-lived but brilliant G. B. Pergolesi (1710—1736). The composer who enjoyed the widest European fame was Adolph Hasse (1699—1783), a German, who began his career as a singer, and learnt the arts of Italian opera under Neapolitan influences, and spread the subtle seductions of its easy fluency with too much success throughout his own country. He married the famous singer Faustina Bordoni. Among the few prominent Italian composers who were not of the Neapolitan school, Steffani (1655—1730), Lotti (1667—1740), Caldara (1678—1768), and Galuppi (1703—1785) honourably represented Venice; and G. Buononcini, Handel's rival, (1672—1752) and Sarti (1729—1802) came from Bologna.

The stiffness and formality of the Italian grand opera were very happily relieved by the influence of the opera buffa and the light pieces called "intermezzi," which were performed between the acts of the grand operas, act for act alternately. Their light humour and gaiety introduced a happy savour of human nature which the solemn and mechanical complacency of the grand opera tended to obliterate. Among the most famous of these was the "Serva Padrona," by Pergolesi, in which the source of much of Mozart's lighter style in the humorous situations of his operas may plainly be traced.

Music in France at this period had no great artistic importance, and only one name of conspicuous interest makes its appearance. J. P. Rameau (1683—1764), the son of the organist of Dijon Cathedral, was intended for the law, but he determined to devote himself to music, and gave his attention at first to musical theory, and wrote an important treatise on the subject. Notwithstanding which, he kept his artistic freshness sufficiently unimpaired to write very successful operas in the later years of his life. His first was "Hippolyte et Aricie," which came out in 1733, and met with great opposition in Paris. "Castor and Pollux" appeared in 1736, and his most important work, "Dardanus," in 1739. He was a man of character and originality, and the genuine verve of his musical ideas cannot be gainsaid. It is shown most happily in the numerous dance tunes with which his operas are interspersed, which show an immense improvement on the standard of Lulli.

About the middle of the century Italian opera buffa was introduced into Paris by an Italian company. It was much opposed on the ground that it was not French, but the French composers imitated the style and improved upon it, and from this source sprang that most successful form, the Opera Comique of later days.

CHAPTER V.

ORATORIO IN THE TIME OF BACH AND HANDEL.

THE Italians enjoyed the distinction of giving the start to Oratorio, as they did to most of the other forms of modern musical art; but, after their composers had developed it to the excellent artistic standard of Carissimi and Stradella, a blight seems to have settled on it, and it rapidly became even more mechanical and pointless than contemporary opera. There were many composers who were fully capable of writing effective and fluent choruses, such as Colonna (1640—1695), Lotti (1667—1740), Durante (1684—1755), and Leo (1694—1746), but they reserved their powers in that line for their Psalms, magnificats, hymns, masses, and motets, and submitted to the public preference for solo singing and fluent melody so far as to reduce the choral part of Oratorios to a minimum, and to seek their effect mainly in strings of formal and conventional arias. It remained, therefore, for other countries to develop this great form of art to its highest standard of interest and artistic completeness.

The mood of Germans was eminently favourable. They had more appreciation of choral effect, and regarded the Oratorio form with much more serious feelings than the Italians. Moreover, it happened that the form which they especially cultivated lent itself naturally to very serious and earnest treatment. Italian Oratorio dealt with a variety of subjects; sometimes Old Testament heroes, sometimes allegorical personages, sometimes famous saints. But German religious intensity showed itself by laying hold cf one subject, and concentrating almost all its fruitful energy on the story of the Passion, as told by the four Evangelists. The source of their treatment of the subject was the traditional mode of reciting the story in Holy week so as to give it more telling effect, by distributing the words of different characters to different readers, and giving the utterances of the masses of people to the choir, which went technically by the name of the "turba." John Walther wrote a musical setting of the tragedy on such lines as early as 1530. Heinrich Schütz followed with a very interesting and expressive treatment of the

"Resurrection" in 1623, and of four "Passions" later in his life. More advanced stages of art are shown in settings by Giovanni Sebastiani in 1672, and Funcke in 1683, and by Keiser in 1703. The art of dramatic choral writing was meanwhile developed in the kindred form of church cantatas, by such masters as Buxtehude, and by John Christoph Bach and John Michael Bach. The Italian aria form was also imitated by German composers, and introduced with effect into the settings of the "Passion"; so that by the time of John Sebastian Bach (1685—1750) the artistic scheme was tolerably complete; and no man was ever more ideally fitted to treat a subject at once mystical and dramatic with the highest intensity and genuine sincerity.

Bach wrote his first setting according to "St. John" in 1723, just before his move from Cöthen to Leipzig (*see* page 42). It was first performed on Good Friday in 1724 at the latter town, soon after he had been appointed cantor of St. Thomas's School and organist of the two principal churches. Beautiful and sincere as this work is, it, however, falls considerably below the great setting of the "Passion" according to St. Matthew, which is far the noblest and most expressive version ever produced. This came out in its first form on Good Friday, 1729, and was afterwards revised and brought out anew in 1740.

In this complete state of the form it is noticeable that it takes the nature rather of a religious exercise than of a mere musical and dramatic entertainment. The story itself occupies comparatively small space, being told in the recitatives allotted to the Evangelist and the other characters, and in the short dramatic outbursts of chorus. What marks the form as ultra-German is the manner in which each step of the tragedy is weighed upon and brought home to the hearer and worshipper by the poetical reflections given either in the form of expressive arias or in the chorales, in which latter the audience (who are thus also worshippers) take part. These are introduced at each step of the story, and serve to emphasise each successive situation; the whole being rounded off by the great reflective choruses which come at the beginning and end of the complete work. In Bach's hands the result is one of the most pathetic and deeply imaginative works in all the range of music. It was too characteristic and serious, even for the German general public of that time; and its performance was restricted to Leipzig in the eighteenth century, and ceased altogether for a time at the beginning of the nineteenth. Mendelssohn revived it at Berlin in 1829, and the first performance in England was that under Sterndale Bennett in 1854. Bach wrote at least two more settings of the "Passion," but they have been lost. The rest of his sacred choral works consists mainly of the numerous church cantatas written for weekly performance in Leipzig, the superb unaccompanied motets, the great B minor Mass, and the so-called Christmas Oratorio written in 1734, which is really a series of cantatas for Christmas Day, New Year's Day, New Year's Sunday, and the Epiphany.

Handel, at the beginning of his career, came under similarly serious influences. He set the "Passion" as early as 1704, and employed in it the highest resources of choral effect and solos. But when he went to Italy he fell in with the Italian taste in Oratorio for a time; and in the two examples of Oratorio which he produced for performance there — the "Resurezzione" and the "Trionfo del Tempo e della Verita"—he reduced the choral portions to a minimum. He nevertheless learnt much from the Italians in the art of smooth and fluent writing for chorus, and put it to excellent use at a later period. When he came to England in 1710 his time was mainly occupied for thirty years in writing and managing operas, but he occasionally wrote serious works, in which choral effect played an important part. He produced the Utrecht "Te Deum" in 1713, and wrote another setting of the "Passion" in 1716, while attending to duties at Hanover. While at Cannons, in the service of the Duke of Chandos as Capellmeister, he produced the "Chandos Anthems," two settings of the "Te Deum," the serenata or masque of "Acis and Galatea," and the first version of "Esther"; which latter appears to have gone at first by the name of "Haman and Mordecai," and to have been described as a masque. This circumstance throws some light on the development of the English oratorio form, which is undoubtedly quite distinct from the Italian form. Masques had been popular at Court in England for many generations. They were a kind of theatrical entertainment in which the interest was more literary than dramatic; and the poem was contrived to serve for a pretty pageant, enhanced by music. The greatest poets had not thought it beneath them to write the poetry for such functions, and they were adorned by the music of the foremost musicians and the scenery and stage management of one at least of the greatest architects. The influence of the associations of this kind of entertainment is seen in the attempts at a national form of opera made in the latter part of the seventeenth century. It also appears to be the principal model upon which the English form of Oratorio was designed. It was a form which was congenial to the English people, who are rather reticent in dramatic matters, and have more taste for choral effect than any other nation, as Handel had very good occasion to observe.

After his short engagement with the Duke of Chandos he resumed his opera career. But in 1731 an independent attempt made by Gates to revive "Esther," with action, caused Handel to revise it and perform it himself, and he also brought "Acis and Galatea" to another hearing with the help of scenery and action. It can hardly be doubted that their success led to an important new departure. At that time he had an opera theatre on his hands and was not allowed to perform secular operas in it on certain days in Lent; and by way of keeping the house employed, he produced in the next year, 1733, the Oratorio of "Deborah" on the stage of his theatre. This was practically his first Oratorio deliberately made as such, and was on the same general lines as the earlier works, "Esther" and "Acis and Galatea." His objects in bringing it forward are patent on the surface. He had to supply the public with an entertainment, and to do it quickly. So he patched together a number of choruses and airs and other movements from earlier works and filled up the spaces with new music, and called the result an Oratorio. The public took very kindly to this form of entertainment, and it proved so much more successful than the operas that he soon followed up "Deborah" with other works of similar cast, such as "Athaliah" (1733) and "Alexander's Feast" (1736). The year 1738 marks the decisive turning of his mind towards the Oratorio form, for in this year he produced both "Saul" and his most monumental work, "Israel in Egypt." Both of these were patched in the same way as "Deborah" had been, but in some respects more unaccountably, for in both he inserted a great deal of music by other people. He probably considered them more as performances to attract an audience than as an artistic expression of his own personal identity, and was not over-sensitive about the materials he used. In "Israel in Egypt" he used music by Stradella, Gaspar Kerl, and Urio, and many movements from a Magnificat which was probably by Erba, though some people cling to the belief that it may be an early work of Handel's own. A great deal of the borrowed portions are distinctly dull, but what remains of Handel's own is so supremely fine that the Oratorio as a whole is likely to be always regarded as Handel's most important achievement.

The end of his opera career came in 1740, and he wrote his most famous work, "The Messiah," in 1741, and brought it to a first hearing in Dublin in 1742. "The Messiah" differs from his other Oratorios in its abstract nature, which seems to make it belong to something of the same category as the German form of Passion music. It is much more of an act of worship or a glorified anthem than a dramatic Oratorio. This also evidently suits English moods, and though it did not lay hold of public taste at once, it seems now to be more firmly rooted in the national affections than any other musical work whatever.

The rest of his Oratorios succeeded each other year by year on the plan of the earlier ones, which clearly approved itself to him, and was, perhaps, too easily handled for their permanent value as wholes. The last was "Jephthah," written in 1751, at a time when his eyesight was already failing. An operation, performed with the hope of restoring his sight, as in the case of J. S. Bach, completely blinded him; but he lingered longer than his great contemporary, and did not leave the world till 1759.

The departure of two such great masters from the scene left the musical world very blank. They had summed up the possibilities of choral music so far, and, till instrumental music had developed a great deal, there was not sufficient field to give another great composer a chance, and the Oratorio form almost completely collapsed for a long time. Arne and Boyce (both born in 1710) produced some artistic Oratorios with distinctly English qualities about them, and Arne left a permanent mark upon the nation by his admirable tunes, such as "Rule, Britannia" (1740), and "Where the bee sucks" (1746). His most successful Oratorio was "Judith" (1773). Arne died in 1778, Boyce in 1779.

In Germany, Philip Emmanuel Bach, who was keenly in sympathy with the modern tendencies of art, and excelled equally in symphonies and sonatas, produced two really interesting Oratorios, "The Israelites in the Desert" (1775) and "The Resurrection and Ascension of Christ" (1787). Both of these works are designed on lines similar to those of the German Passions, and both are most significant in the qualities which show the progress of the art of instrumentation: and a treatment of chorus which is more in kinship with the harmonic tendencies of modern times than with the grand and characteristic elaboration of his great father's work.

In Italy Oratorio ceased to have any significance, and Church music became for the most part conventional and operatic. Italian composers wrote fluent counterpoint in their choruses, but their Church works have a singular lack of point and character. Besides those mentioned at the beginning of the chapter a few merit reference. Astorga (1681—1736) for his charmingly musical and expressive "Stabat Mater"; Marcello (1686—1739) for his famous Psalms; Pergolesi (1710—1736) for his "Stabat Mater," &c.

CHAPTER VI.

THE PROGRESS OF INSTRUMENTAL MUSIC UP TO THE TIME OF J. S. BACH.

THE history of Instrumental Music divides naturally into three well-defined periods. The first extends from the early experiments in the fifteenth and sixteenth centuries up to the time of J. S. Bach, the second up to Beethoven, and the third till the present day. They are each marked by consistent distinguishing traits. The first by contrapuntal methods akin to those of choral music ; the second by the development of pure harmonic forms of the sonata order, which are shown in their highest perfection in the sonatas and symphonies of Beethoven; and the third by a striving after greater freedom than the pure sonata forms seem to allow, or an extension of its scheme by intellectual devices, and new kinds of contrapuntal methods ; or by more decisive adoption than formerly of ideas and programmes as the basis of art.

In the early days of the first of these periods modern instruments were not available. The stringed instruments played with bows were the various Viols—treble, mean, tenor, viola da gamba, and violone or double bass. And for this set a quantity of music, both in the shape of dance tunes and of movements copied from choral canzonas and similar choral works was written. Lutes of various sizes were conspicuously popular and useful, and the style of music written for them has permeated many types of more modern music written for other instruments. The position occupied by the pianoforte was held by the harpsichord and the clavichord, and an immense quantity of music of permanent value was written for them in various countries.

All the forms of instrumental music then known throve in England in the time of the Stuarts, as has been described above in the second chapter. The last and greatest representative of this early English school was Henry Purcell, who had the advantage of knowing something of French and Italian models. His most important instrumental compositions are the Suites or Lessons for harpsichord and two sets of Sonatas for strings. The first of these sets of Sonatas was published in his lifetime, in 1684; and the second by his widow, in 1697. These Sonatas are on the regular Italian plan familiar in Corelli's works; the most celebrated is that known as the Golden Sonata, which is No. 9 of the second set; many others have fully as interesting qualities. The admirable dance music he wrote for various plays ought also to be counted as representative of his skill as an instrumental composer. The movements are remarkably full of variety and point for the time when they were written.

Instrumental music throve also in France in those days, and early showed distinctive traits. The familiar inclination of the French for expressing their feelings by gestures has its counterpart in their predominant taste for dance rhythms in music and their love for ballet on the stage. Their own particular form of opera, which was set going by Cambert and Lulli, was mainly founded on ballet and kindred kinds of stage effect. Lulli no doubt gave considerable impulse to French instrumental music by the profusion of dance tunes he wrote for his operas. And he did good service to art by the type and style of overture he adopted, which was followed by Handel in the overtures to his operas and oratorios, and by other composers in the same line even in quite modern times, such as Spohr and Mendelssohn.

The department of instrumental music in which the French specially excelled was that of music for the harpsichord. Among the early masters was Jacques Champion de Chambonnières, who was harpsichordist to Louis XIV. in the early part of his reign, and published harpsichord music in 1670. A collection of "Pièces de Clavecin," by Le Bégue, also deserves mention, which was published in Paris in 1677. The greatest of the French school was François Couperin (1668—1733). He wrote a profusion of little movements, full of grace, fancy, and character, grouped into sets called "Ordres," such as are now commonly called Suites. He showed his most solid gifts in his allemandes, sarabandes, and preludes, and his lighter and more popular vein in his rondos, and the numbers of pieces with fanciful names which generally formed the latter part of these "Ordres." He is the prototype of an essentially French school, which has continued till the present day to supply the world with little pieces based on some dance rhythm, or a title which explains and supplies the motive of the pieces. The type is evidently more congenial to their taste for effect and natural vivacity than the forms of abstract instrumental music. Couperin also wrote a book called "L'Art de toucher le Clavecin" (1717), which is a most invaluable and complete explanation of harpsichord playing in its prime, and is often referred to by him in editions of his compositions as "Ma Méthode." Similar to Couperin's works are the many pieces for harpsichord by J. P. Rameau (1683—1764). His first "Book of pieces for the Clavecin" came out in 1706. The plan of his suites is much the same as Couperin's, comprising a few solid movements at the beginning and a number of lively tunes and rondos in the latter part. There is even more directness and point about some of Rameau's picture-tunes than Couperin's, and the connection with the stage is more obvious, inasmuch as some of those which are still familiar to modern pianists appear also as ballet pieces in his operas.

Before the end of the sixteenth century organs had arrived at a fairly complete state. It was natural that the associations of the organ should cause organists to imitate choral works in their compositions; and they improved upon them first by introducing a great variety of turns and runs and ornaments. These ultimately developed into a special kind of composition, somewhat like the product of extemporisation, consisting mainly of runs, accompanied by simple successions of chords. This form was commonly known as a Toccata; and though crude and elementary, it has considerable historical importance as one of the first of the large musical forms which established a sort of individuality, as an instrumental composition independent of choral models. Its earliest representative composers were Andrea Gabrieli (1510—1586), and his famous nephew, Giovanni Gabrieli (1557—1612), and Claudio Merulo (1533—1604), all of whom were organists of St Mark's at Venice. The most important of the early northern organists was Jan Pieterszoon Sweelinck, organist of Amsterdam (1562—1621). His work, consisting of fugues, variations, toccatas, is marked by a considerable inventive gift, and talent for speculation, which were remarkably helpful to the progress of his branch of the art. He was the prototype of the northern group of organists, some of whom, especially Reinken, were among the models of John Sebastian Bach. The greatest of the early organists, and the first who arrived at any real maturity of style, was Girolamo Frescobaldi (1583—1644), organist of St. Peter's at Rome. His works comprise some of the earliest examples of well-developed

THE PROGRESS OF INSTRUMENTAL MUSIC. 39

fugues of the modern kind, as well as specimens of all the forms known in his time, which show that he had great mastery of resource and inventiveness, as well as firm grasp of artistic principles.

The earliest of the great German organists was S. Scheidt, born in Halle in 1587. He wrote a large quantity of remarkable music for his instrument, and died 1654. Soon after him came Frescobaldi's pupil, Froberger, who was born early in the seventeenth century, and died 1667. He was even more important as a writer of harpsichord music than for his organ music; since he adapted the methods of the organ composers to the smaller domestic instrument, and was a special prototype of J. S. Bach in that respect. Gaspar Kerl, who is thought to have been a pupil of Carissimi and of Frescobaldi, was born in 1628. He wrote good choral music as well as organ music. One of his organ canzonas was imported bodily by Handel into "Israel in Egypt." Johann Pachelbel (1653—1706) was organist of St. Sebald in Nuremberg, and one of Bach's models for organ composition. Reinken (1623—1722), another very remarkable organist and composer, was a pupil of Sweelinck; the Danish organist, Buxtehude (1637—1707) also exercised considerable influence on J. S. Bach.

The most important and fruitful line of instrumental music emerged from the obscurity of indefinite experiment into the light of a promising dawn in Italy in the latter part of the seventeenth century. The name with which the decisive awakening of violin music to life is always rightly associated is that of Arcangelo Corelli (1653—1713). In his time the art of violin making was brought to perfection. Nicolo Amati was his senior by many years, and Antonio Straduarius and Joseph Guarnerius, the two greatest of violin makers, were his contemporaries. Corelli represents the essentially solid and expressively musical school of violin playing. He was in nowise greatly expert in mechanical difficulties, but the traditions of his solid style have been handed down from master to pupil through successive generations of famous players till the present day. His works consist entirely of sonatas and concertos for stringed instruments, with accompaniment of figured bass for archlute, or harpsichord, or organ. The first set, consisting of twelve "Sonate da Chiesa," was published in Rome in 1683; the second set, twelve "Sonate da Camera," in 1685. The distinction between these Church and

Chamber sonatas is important, since the former represents (in an antiquated disguise) the modern abstract sonata, while the latter represents the dance suite. The type of the Church sonata is a set of four movements—(1) a slow introductory movement, (2) a canzona or fugal movement, (3) a short slow movement, (4) a lively rhythmic movement. The Chamber sonatas commonly begin with an introductory slow movement, followed by a solid allemande, corrente, sarabande, and generally have a lively giga or gavotte to conclude with. The whole of his compositions amount to no more than five sets of such sonatas and a set of concertos. What gives them their permanent attraction is their artistic equality and fluency, combined with simplicity, sweetness, a vein of poetic expression, dignity, and an admirably even flow of easy part-writing. Corelli was in no sense the inventor of this form of art, as it was obviously familiar to many composers before his time and contemporary with him; but he set the seal of an evenly-balanced individuality upon his works in such a manner as to make them one of the landmarks of musical history.

Immediately after his time the great Italian school of violinists bloomed into wonderful vigour and perfection—several of Corelli's own pupils occupying an important position among them, such as Somis (1676—1763), Locatelli (1693—1764), and Geminiani (1680—1761). Other great players, more or less independent of Corelli, also made their appearance, such as Veracini (1685—1750) and Vivaldi (born in the latter part of the seventeenth century, died 1743), and Tartini (1692—1770). The school continued to flourish till the days of Mozart and Beethoven, and their works and deeds belong mostly to the second period of instrumental music, as their compositions are mainly of the sonata kind, and illustrate harmonic principles. Vivaldi, however, occupied a peculiar position, both as the early representative of the brilliant school of players and as a writer of a great number of concertos for stringed instruments, which served as the models to J. S. Bach for his compositions of that description. Vivaldi was very early among those who had a strong sense of the value of simple relations of tonic and dominant as a principle of design, and had the ability to use such contrasts systematically and effectively.

Among early German violinists must be mentioned H. J. F. von Biber (1638—1698). He was a famous performer and a worthy composer, and published a set of sonatas as early as 1681.

Handel's position in respect of instrumental music is comparatively unimportant. His most famous instrumental composition is the first set of lessons or suites, which came out in 1720. As types of the "Suite" form they are irregular, and combine features both of church and chamber sonatas of the Italian kind. The former is illustrated by the number of fugues, which correspond to the canzonas in the early church sonatas; while interspersed with regular accepted dance tunes are sets of variations, which are unusual features in such works. The next most familiar are his violin sonatas and his organ concertos, which are mainly on Italian lines, and in their way admirable. The least familiar are his many concertos for orchestral instruments, which again are based on Italian models, and do not look as if he had taken much pains with them. Several are made up for occasions out of movements from other works, such as oratorios and operas; and movements have sometimes been used at least three times in different works. They are generally instinct with Handel's usual vigour and breadth, but occupy no very important position in musical history.

The position of J. S. Bach in relation to instrumental music is in strong contrast to that of Handel. Handel wrote most of his instrumental music for occasions, Bach chiefly to find the most perfect artistic expression of his ideas in the various forms of instrumental art existing in his time. He studied the works of all the recognised masters of different schools so minutely and carefully that his works became the sum of all the development hitherto attempted in instrumental music. He always applied himself in accordance with his opportunities. In his younger days, when organist of various towns, such as Lüneburg, Arnstadt, Mühlhausen, he studied organ works and the performances of Buxtehude and Reinken, and Georg Boehm. In his first important post as organist at Weimar, he composed the greater part of his famous organ works, and some of his best Church cantatas. When, in 1717, he was made Capellmeister to the Prince of Anhalt Cöthen, who had a special taste for instrumental music, he devoted himself specially to that branch of art, and it was at that time that most of his important work in instrumental music was done. He gave his attention to Vivaldi's concertos and copied out and rearranged sixteen of them for practice; and the outcome of this labour is shown in the fine set of six called the Brandenburg Concertos, which were written for the Markgraf of

Brandenburg and sent to him in 1721. And to the same influence must be traced the well known Italian Concerto for clavier and the Concerto for two violins in D, and other similar productions of the time when he was at Cöthen. It was also during this time (in 1722) that he completed the first half of the work known to all musicians as the Forty-eight Preludes and Fugues. This consisted of a collection of twenty-four pieces, written at various times, and brought together under the name of " Das Wohltemperirte Clavier," which means a clavier tuned in equal temperament, so that all keys are equally available instead of some being out of tune in order that a few others may be more particularly in tune; and Bach evidently meant to express his adherence to such tuning in preference to the older method by writing this set of pieces in all keys both major and minor. At Cöthen he also wrote his violin sonatas and the Suites Françaises. In 1723 he moved to his last important post of Cantor at the St. Thomas School and Organist of St. Thomas and St. Nicholas churches in Leipzig. For the remainder of his life there he was mainly occupied with great choral works, such as the Passions, the Great Mass and the Church cantatas, but he still gave much attention to instrumental music. The English Suites were completed by 1726, and the publication of the Partitas, which had begun in 1726, was completed in 1731. Of the three sets of Suites the French are the lightest and brightest, the English the most solid, and the Partitas the most varied; and the whole series stands in the same relation to suite music of all times as Beethoven's sonatas stand to all music of that class. The twenty-four preludes and fugues constituting the second book of the Wohltemperirte Clavier (making up the complete forty-eight) were finally collected together in 1740, eighteen years after the first book. The collection represents the accumulation of pieces which had probably been going on for years, as Bach's constant habit was to revise again and again till he got his work near enough to his own standard of artistic perfection.

In all Bach's most successful instrumental compositions his leaning towards the methods of the old school is evident. The elasticity and expansiveness of such old forms as the Fugue, the Canzona, the Toccata, and the early type of Fantasia made them more attractive to him than the Sonata types, which seemed to limit the range of harmony and modulation. He very rarely attempted anything important in regular Sonata form, and when he did the result is not very characteristic of him. He must therefore be regarded rather as the culminating representative of the polyphonic period of instrumental music than the forerunner of the harmonic period, whose representatives, until Beethoven's time, almost ignored both his music and his principles.

Among composers who distinguished themselves in Germany in the early stages of instrumental music the following must also be remembered: Johann Kuhnau (1677—1722), Bach's predecessor as Cantor of St. Thomas School, who wrote both sonatas and suites, and was a man of law and learning; Johann Mattheson (1681—1722), Handel's friend, who wrote suites and several very valuable works on music; August Gottlieb Muffat, born about 1690 and died in 1742, wrote a large quantity of harpsichord music of various kinds. And the survey will not be complete without reference to that unique figure, the Italian, Domenico Scarlatti (1683—1757). He was a son of the famous Alessandro, and in the earlier part of his life followed much the same career as his father, writing operas and church music. The direction in which his special gifts of harpsichord playing lay was not fully appreciated by Italians, but after 1721 he settled in Lisbon, and found there and at Madrid a congenial audience among the people of the Court; and it was this encouragement which induced him to produce the mass of his harpsichord music. Only thirty pieces were published in his lifetime, under the name of "Exercises for the Gravicembalo"; but altogether he produced several hundreds. In later times they are always spoken of as sonatas, and for their self-dependent nature they are rightly so named, though they only consist of one movement apiece. They are remarkable as among the first works of the kind in which neither the fugue principle nor dance rhythm are essential features. They are based on very definite ideas and a grouping of keys similar to that found in modern sonata movements of the completely harmonic type; and his manner of repeating phrases again and again has its counterpart in Mozart's works. His instinct for his instrument was extremely acute, and his devices of execution have been imitated by great writers for the pianoforte up to the most recent times.

CHAPTER VII.

THE PROGRESS OF INSTRUMENTAL MUSIC IN THE EIGHTEENTH CENTURY.

It is from the Italians that our modern style of instrumental music springs. Their inclination for simplicity of design and for easing the labour of attention seems to have led them, first of all people, to cultivate those simple kinds of harmonic contrast upon which the whole system of modern instrumental music rests. The contrapuntal style of art which culminated in the works of Bach and Handel was full of vigour and variety, but it showed signs of being toned down into more easy and obvious moods, in the choral works of even such early Italian masters as Leo, Durante, and Colonna; and this tendency is shown in a more marked degree in instrumental works such as the Concertos of Vivaldi. Early in the eighteenth century composers of Italian operas and of Italian instrumental music moved in the same direction. The writers of operas simplified their airs to the utmost to satisfy the taste of their indolent audiences. They made them as much as possible on one uniform pattern, in which simple contrast of the harmonies of tonic and dominant was essential to success; and they planned their overtures and preliminary symphonies on much the same principles. The great school of Italian violinists, whose artistic aims were much higher and nobler, were insensibly drawn in the same direction, and conveyed their ideas more and more in uniform harmonic designs. Some of them introduced allemandes and gigas, and other movements more characteristic of suites, into their sonatas, but even these soon became more and more harmonic in character and more distinctly uniform in plan. In Corelli (1653—1713) the contrapuntal style was still predominant; in the works of his pupils and immediate successors the balance began to lean towards the harmonic style. Passages founded on chords made more and more frequent appearance in them, and so did those figures of accompaniment which are among its most decisive indications.

The great school of Italian violinists came to its zenith very quickly. Corelli's style was noble and pure, but his technical resources were undoubtedly limited. His immediate successors extended the technical resources of the instrument, and adopted a much more modern style of expression. The eldest of his most famous pupils was Somis (1676—1763), who was born in Piedmont, and became a pupil first of Corelli and afterwards of Vivaldi. He settled in Turin, and is considered the head of the Piedmontese School. Among Somis' most famous pupils was the Frenchman Le Clair (1697—1764), who began life as a ballet master and writer of ballet music. He attracted Somis' attention while acting in that capacity at Turin, and under his guidance developed into a great violinist. Nevertheless he had not the good fortune to win any high position as a player, though he left some admirable sonatas of the Italian type. A more famous pupil of Corelli's was Geminiani (1680—1761), a man of great abilities, but gifted with a temperament so excitable and ill-regulated that it prevented his attaining the position as a performer which his powers seemed to warrant. He, however, immensely enlarged the technique of the instrument, both by his compositions—such as sonatas and concertos—and by his teaching. His compositions were considered extremely difficult, and are not exactly child's-play even now, despite the advances made in technique; and they often present strikingly modern features of harmonization and expression. He also wrote a very valuable book on violin-playing which was far ahead of its time. He came to England in 1714, and spent a great part of his life here. One of Geminiani's most famous pupils was the Englishman Dubourg (1703—1767), who from 1728 was leader of the Viceroy's band in Dublin, and in that capacity led the orchestra on the occasion of the first performance of "The Messiah," in 1741. It was in his house that Geminiani died. Another famous pupil of Corelli's was Locatelli (1693—1764), who was born in Bergamo, settled in manhood at Amsterdam, and made a great reputation as a virtuoso. Some of his compositions are often blamed for artificial effects which are purely eccentric; but he was also capable of writing really admirable music, as his violin sonatas sufficiently prove.

In the same generation appeared, according to report, one of the greatest violinists of the world. This was Giuseppe

Tartini (1692—1770). He was a Florentine by birth, and first studied law, but some matrimonial complications caused him to hide for two years in a monastery at Assisi, during which time he devoted himself to music and taught himself the violin. Soon after leaving the monastery he happened to hear Veracini in Venice, and was so struck with his own shortcomings by comparison that he went to work again for another two years in Ancona. Padua ultimately became his home. He was a man of large feeling and cultivated mind. As a player his style is said to have been particularly noble and expressive, and his sonatas of the Italian type—thoroughly harmonic in plan— are the best of all that fine group of highly artistic works ; especially the famous "Trillo del Diavolo," and the one in G minor known as " Didone abandonnata." Tartini was one of the first musicians to draw attention to some acoustical phenomena known as " combination tones," which he called " Terzi tuoni." His influence was mingled with the direct Corellian traditions through his pupil Pugnani (1727—1803), who was also a pupil of Somis. This famous violinist and teacher was born in Piedmont, and travelled in many European countries giving concerts. He wrote a good deal of violin music, and had a very famous pupil in the person of Viotti (1753—1824). Viotti was also of Piedmont, and studied under Pugnani in Turin. Later he travelled with him, and after that settled for some time in Paris, occupying himself mainly with teaching ; for, though an extraordinarily fine performer, he greatly disliked playing in public. When the French Revolution came to its crisis, he crossed over to England, and led at various concerts in London, including some of those at which Haydn's symphonies were first performed. He is particularly notable for the large quantity of violin music he wrote, comprising concertos, quartets, duos, &c., which, though not of any great mark as actual music, are so admirably suited to the nature of the instrument and range over so wide a variety of technique that they are particularly valuable for teaching purposes.

His pupils, Rode (1774—1830) and Baillot (1771—1842), were famous representatives of the French branch of this school, all of whose members occupy an honourable position in the history of art and did most valuable service in furthering it.

In the department of clavier sonata, the Italians were not so prominent, since their best composers of instrumental music were more attracted by the singing qualities of the violin. But they exerted much influence on its character and history, partly because the operatic style was more frequently used by composers of clavier sonatas than violin sonatas. The great Italian violinists wrote their sonatas for themselves to play; the writers of clavier music too often wrote their sonatas for fashionable pupils, whose tastes were mainly in the operatic direction. In the generation after the famous Domenico Scarlatti Italy was fairly well represented. The opera composer Galuppi wrote many sonatas for clavier, which have excellent points, and another of the best writers of the early clavier sonatas was Paradisi (1710—1792), who was born in Naples, but settled in London, where he brought out a successful opera, "Phaeton," and a set of sonatas for "gravicembalo," as the harpsichord was sometimes called. Among these are some of the best examples of the early sonatas—neat, elegant, finished, and well balanced, and very clear and complete in form. Of less enviable fame is Alberti (died 1740), an amateur and a good singer, who published a set of sonatas which became popular. These contained such a profuse amount of one particular formula of accompaniment that it has been generally known in later years as the Alberti bass.

The clavier sonata was cultivated with greater musical success by the Germans. They, in their turn, were not so highly successful as violinists, and rather preferred the keyed instruments; perhaps because they were less attracted to melody than to harmony. Bach's sons and pupils were specially distinguished for their works of this order. More especially the second son, Carl Philip Emmanuel (1714—1788). Like all the representatives of his generation, he was affected to a certain degree by the Italian influence, springing from the universal popularity of the Italian opera throughout Europe. But he kept more of the artistic vigour and genuineness of his father than any of his brothers and contemporaries. He wrote an immense number of sonatas, which are the best representative works of their kind in the interval between the days of Bach and Handel and the time of Haydn; and it was his sonatas which Haydn specially studied in early years as models for his own efforts in the same line. He also wrote some very curious, and sometimes interesting, experimental works, in a fantasia form, full of abrupt changes of time and strange modulations, and long passages without any bars; also some excellent and vigorous symphonies, which are original in design and contain some very characteristic instrumentation. He was altogether a man of high intelligence and honourable purpose, and contributed, among his other services to art, an invaluable treatise on the way to play keyed instruments. His youngest brother, John Christian Bach (1735—1782), also made a considerable mark as a composer of instrumental music. He was only fifteen when his father died, and felt his influence least among the brothers. He went early to Italy and was for a time organist of Milan Cathedral. Later he settled in England and obtained a great position, both as a fashionable teacher and as a composer of sonatas, symphonies, and operas. His style was ultra-Italian. He is sometimes called the English Bach and sometimes the Milanese Bach. He exerted considerable influence on Mozart, who made friends with him when he came to England as a youthful prodigy. Many other composers added to the enormous mass of clavier music without greatly furthering the cause of art, though without discredit to themselves. Some few clung to the traditions of the ancient school, and wrote solid works of the suite order, and toccatas and fantasias and fugues; such as Krebs (1713—1780), one of Bach's favourite pupils, and Eberlin (1702—1776).

Meanwhile a much larger and more important form of art was progressing to maturity. In the next generation the general progress of mastery of design and instrumental resource advanced the standard of clavier sonatas and brought into being other forms of solo compositions, such as quartets, trios, &c. But the phases of progress which appear in them are all comprised in the progress of the grand form of the symphony, which is the highest and purest art-form of modern music.

The ultimate rise of this form of Art was in the instrumental movements which were used for the overtures of operas. These were at first very short, and little more than simple and somewhat pointless successions of chords. By the latter part of the seventeenth century they had developed into a group of movements something like the group which at that time frequently constituted sonatas and concertos. In Alessandro Scarlatti's time this "Sinfonia avanti l'opera" consisted of either three or four short movements, alternately slow and fast; and the order adopted uniformly by almost all composers soon after was a group of three, consisting of—first, a solid

THE PROGRESS OF INSTRUMENTAL MUSIC. 49

allegro, then a short slow movement, and lastly a light and lively allegro. In course of time these groups of movements began to attract some little attention, and as they improved in musical interest and artistic completeness they were often played apart from the operas. They were found very serviceable in this independent form, and to meet the demand an enormous number were produced by all manner of composers. They were usually scored for a group of eight instruments— that is, the complete set of strings and two pairs of wind instruments, such as two horns and two hautboys, or two horns and two flutes. Sometimes they were published as "overtures in eight parts," as were Abel's and John Christian Bach's, and sometimes as "symphonies in eight parts," as were Michael Esser's, Wagenseil's, Richter's, &c. The difference in name implies no difference in the works; as they might or might not have originally been attached to an opera. The quality of the music was for the most part very flat, common, and empty, and very little attempt was made at either refined phrasing or effects of instrumentation. But every now and then a composer tried to put something genuine into his work, and a most important step was taken by the violinist and composer Stamitz (1719—1761). He became leader and conductor of the band of the Elector of Mannheim in the early half of the century, and, being evidently a man of taste, set about making the performance more refined and artistic. Burney speaks of him as discovering the effect of crescendo and diminuendo, "and that the *piano*, which before was chiefly used as an echo, as well as the *forte*, had their shades as well as red and blue in painting." From which it may be divined that in the dreary period between J. S. Bach and Haydn music of this kind had been played in a most slatternly manner. The effect of Stamitz's reform was very great. The Mannheim band won the reputation of being the best in Europe, and kept up its standard of excellence long enough (after Stamitz's death) to exert a very powerful influence on Mozart.

In point of form all these early symphonies were distinctly harmonic, representing the same scheme as the movements of modern sonatas, with but trifling deviations. In the hands of German composers the primitive outline of the design was enriched by degrees and developed to a more artistic standard of interest. Carl Philip Emmanuel Bach alone took a line of his own, which was more akin to his father's method in concertos. He commonly adopted some striking principle of effect as his cue, and alternated his subjects irregularly, distributing the modulations on quite different principles from those in his sonata movements, except in so far as the movements made digressions from the starting key, and returned to it finally at the conclusion to establish the unity. His material, at all events in the symphonies of 1772, is immensely more vigorous and animated than that of his contemporaries, and his treatment of instruments original and often ingenious. In the end his manner of dealing with form was abandoned by other composers for the sonata type, which was almost universally adopted. In that respect his younger brother, John Christian, stands more in the direct line of the descent of modern symphony, though his musical material is less vigorous. However, he had some excellent ideas of orchestral effect, and similar gifts were shown by the Belgian Gossec (1733—1829), who pushed the cause of instrumental music vigorously in Paris in the middle and latter half of the century.

But all these numerous early writers of symphonies were completely put in the background before the end of the century by Haydn and Mozart.

A few points of Haydn's early career bear on the history of the art. He was born at Rohrau, a small village in Austria, in 1732. His father was a wheelwright and his mother a cook in the service of Count Harrach; so he was altogether a son of the people. He entered the choir of St. Stephen's Church, in Vienna, under Reutter, in 1740, and stayed there till his voice broke, in 1745, when he was sent off to provide for himself. He took to composing early, and studied the clavier sonatas of Philip Emmanuel Bach as models. He was appointed Capellmeister to a Bohemian count, Morzin, in 1759, and began in that same year to write symphonies. His first attempts were precisely on the lines of those above described, and in no sense markedly distinct in style. When his connection with Count Morzin came to an end, he had the good fortune to be engaged as Capellmeister by Prince Anton Esterhazy, a Hungarian noble of immense wealth, who had a palace near Eisenstadt in which he kept an orchestra, chorus, solo singers, and all the appurtenances needful for grand musical performances. Prince Anton died in 1762, but his brother, Nicolaus, kept Haydn on and gave him every encouragement by his thorough sympathy with his art. This prince soon after moved to the still more magnificent palace of Esterhaz, where Haydn's opportunities were such as rarely fall to the lot of a composer. He had a theatre, a band always ready to play his new works, and a sympathetic and intelligent audience. For the prince and his guests he wrote an immense number of symphonies, and found encouragement to make them more artistic, by raising the standard of the ideas and developing the resources of orchestral effect; and by degrees his fame began to spread abroad. But he did not come to the perfection of his mastery of this great form of art till Mozart had come and completed his share of active work and passed away.

Mozart was also of South German stock. He was born at Salzburg in 1756, and began to show his astounding powers soon after he could walk. His wise father fostered them with great wisdom, and by the time he was five he composed the music for a comedy by Eberlin, the composer, which was performed in his native town. When he was seven he started on a sort of triumphal progress to the principal capitals of Europe, appearing in the character both of performer and composer. After going to Vienna, Italy, and Paris, he came to England, and here, at the age of eight, he composed his first symphonies. His early instrumental compositions show a remarkable breadth and mastery of style, but it was not till less happy and successful days that he began to show the real high qualities of his genius in the line of orchestral symphonies. In 1777 and 1778, when he was twenty-one and on his way to Paris to try and improve his position by getting works performed there, he stayed at Mannheim for some time, and there came into contact with the refined and artistic traditions of Stamitz in respect of orchestral performances. It is clear that this gave him a new insight into the possibilities of orchestral effect, and it bore fruit in the remarkably fine symphony (in D) which he wrote soon after in Paris, the first which shows his mature powers of orchestration. It happens to be the most fully scored of all his symphonies, and shows a gift for realising orchestral colour which was then new to the world. Altogether he wrote forty-nine symphonies; but those which mark the full degree of his powers are comparatively few. The most noteworthy after the Parisian Symphony of 1778 are a particularly fine one which he wrote for Prague in 1786 (the year when "Figaro" came out) and the three greatest of all in E flat, G minor, and C, which he wrote in

Vienna in 1788, and which are the crown of his symphonic works, if not indeed of all his works. The advance that they indicate beyond anything of a symphonic kind which had appeared up to that time in the world is almost beyond computation.   They seem like an art-type of almost a different era. Mozart was indeed the first composer born in the world endowed with the complete aptitudes requisite for abstract instrumental music ; having both a high and delicate sense of orchestral colour and an exceptional mastery of form.   In these last symphonies he shows the true elasticity in handling and grouping his instruments— artistic variety, perfect management of degrees of light and shade, and unfailing sense of proportion, which, combined with the ready flow of ideas of various moods, make an art-product of the highest degree of perfection.   The rest of his short life was occupied with writing the " *Zauberflöte* " and other operas, and the " Requiem," and he had no further opportunity to attempt symphonies before he left the world in December, 1791.

In his early days Mozart might have learnt from Haydn ; in the latter part of his life Haydn learnt, right willingly, from him. Haydn's fame by about the end of Mozart's life had become universal, and several efforts had been made to induce him to come to England ; but he would not desert his master or his duties.   Ultimately, in 1790, Prince Esterhazy died, and Haydn was persuaded by the violinist Salomon to come to this country and compose symphonies for a series of concerts which that enterprising man proposed to give in London ; and then it was that the twelve symphonies which are the crowning glory of Haydn's life-work were written. His long experience and the example of Mozart lifted him to his highest level, and he produced for this country the series which mark to the full all the natural geniality, humour, vigour, and   simple good-heartedness which were his characteristics, in those terms of perfect art which, though not so delicately poised and finished as Mozart's, are fair parallels in point of artistic management. Six of them were written for his first visit in 1791, and the rest for his second visit in 1794.   He lived some time after this, but was occupied with other lines of work, and died in 1809 without adding further to the store of his symphonic achievements.

The nature of the change which had been effected in the symphony since Haydn began to write may be summarised.

THE PROGRESS OF INSTRUMENTAL MUSIC. 53

In his early days it was a type of rather slight artistic importance. The ideas used were generally rather vapid, the design of the movements simple but uninteresting, the group of instruments used small, and the method of their employment blunt and crude. By the time Haydn and Mozart arrived at the climax of their work the group of instruments was much more highly organised, the element of powerful tone in trumpets and drums had been added, and the group of wood-wind was expanded in many cases to the full variety of flutes, hautboys, clarinets, and bassoons, which is familiar in the full modern orchestra. Both composers used clarinets rarely, but they knew how to use them with effect. The whole treatment of the orchestral forces had become transformed. In early times the wind instruments were occasionally used for solo purposes, and often did no more than crudely fill up and reinforce the mass of sound; but in their later symphonies they were used with much more independence, as well as with far more coherence and sense of balance. Then the ideas and subjects themselves had attained to a much more definite character and a much higher degree of beauty and individuality; and the resources of modulation had been applied to enhance and give extra variety and interest to the designs of the movements. The old number of three movements had in many cases been increased to four, and the relation of the movements to one another in point of contrast as well as coherence of style had become artistically perfect. It only remained for Beethoven to apply all these elements of art to the expression of a higher range of ideas and completely to balance the idea and the form in which the idea was expressed, so as to make one of the most perfect forms of art the world has ever seen.

The connection of Haydn and Mozart with the development of the clavier sonata and such forms of solo art as the quartet are of great importance, and the progress they made moves on parallel lines with that of the symphony. In the clavier sonata the improvement made by them was mainly in the matter of design; for before their time a group of only two movements was common, and the design of the movements was at once less concise and less interesting than it had become at the end of the century. But the improvements made were not by any means only owing to them. A very large proportion of their sonatas were of but slight importance, and were probably written for the use of pupils;

and a lack of decided musical purpose in them makes them on an average of less historical importance than either Philip Emmanuel Bach's work in their own time or Domenico Scarlatti's in the earlier time. The progress of the type of works for keyed instruments has been always rather dependent on the feeling for effect which composers, who were also performers, gained from their practical experiences; and Haydn and Mozart, being limited by the nature of the instrument for which they wrote, which was mainly the harpsichord, did not expand the limits of the form so notably as they did in other branches. It was not till the improvement of the pianoforte came about that the new and richer opportunities for effect thereby offered gave a fresh spur to the development of this form of art.

With the quartet for solo strings the case was different; such a form hardly existed before their time, and their work with it was such as almost to complete its artistic maturity in the course of one generation. As a domestic form of high-class art quartets had had parallels in contrapuntal days in the "consorts for viols," "fantasias of various parts," and suites and Sonate da Camera and Sonate da Chiesa for similar groups of instruments. But in them the pleasure of the player was more studied than that of the auditor, and a fatal defect was the absence of any appropriate type of abstract form which was suitable for music without words. The growth of the system of harmonic design, and the development of the technique of the violin, were the causes that brought about the perfecting of the quartet and kindred forms of chamber music. Haydn's first quartet was written in 1755. It was of slender proportions and no great interest. But he soon infused vigour and artistic value into his later works of the kind, giving the instruments more and more independence, and finding how to express more with such simple means. He continued composing them all through his life and was actually engaged on one when his powers finally broke down with failing health in old age. Mozart took up the form at a higher level, and though he did not do so much for its earlier development, he set even a nobler seal upon it in the superb group of six which he wrote in 1782 and dedicated to Haydn. It shows how great an advance they represent upon the average standard of the time that they were generally received with dislike even rising to indignation. To later generations they appear as perfect in artistic moderation as they are in mastery of design and skill in the use of the four solo instruments. Mozart wrote a few others later, which were not considered so abstruse, and are equally artistic. There were several other composers who did good service in Haydn's time in the development of the quartet form; notably Boccherini (1740—1805), who was a native of Lucca, and early made a great reputation as a composer and violinist. His facility in composition was extraordinary, and he produced altogether over 360 instrumental compositions, of which a large number are quartets and quintets. The German Dittersdorf (1738—1799) was a most voluminous and successful composer in every branch of art, and among his various works are many quartets of slight and simple style, but excellently written and artistically balanced.

The progress of modern instrumental music caused it to branch off into various lines, such as concertos, divertimenti, overtures, and numerous varieties of chamber music; but these all developed in their respective lines parallel to the greater and more central types to which they are akin; each received good measure of attention from the greatest composers, and before the end of the century progressed from the cruder types of the early days into most finished and artistic products. The most important phases of development being in all cases the improvement of design, and the more appropriate, independent, and characteristic use of the instruments. The highest phase of all in instrumental music had still to wait till the early years of the nineteenth century for its consummation.

CHAPTER VIII.

OPERA IN GLUCK AND MOZART'S TIME, AND IMMEDIATELY AFTER.

ABOUT the middle of the eighteenth century the indolence of fashionable audiences and the short-sighted egotism of popular singers had reduced the opera to such a state of monotonous and mechanical dulness that a reaction was inevitable. Slight changes and improvements were frequently attempted by various composers, but the name with which the most definite attempts at general reform are always associated is that of C. Willibald von Gluck.

This notable composer was born at Neumarkt in Germany in 1714, and was early subjected to Italian influences; as he first went to Vienna (where Italian taste was predominant) in 1736, and then completed his musical studies in Milan, where he brought out his first Italian opera, "Artaserse," in 1741. Meeting with success in this work he followed it up with several more of the usual Italian pattern, such as "Demofoon," "Artamene," "Poro," "Alessandro nell' Indie." He was invited to England in 1745, just at the time that Handel was in the full swing of his Oratorio career. Gluck did not make a great mark in England, but he had the advantage of hearing Handel's solid choral works, and the impression made on him was doubtless one of the causes which led him to break away from the vapid traditions of the old opera seria. A still more powerful cause was the impression made on him by Rameau's operas, which he heard in Paris on his way back to Vienna from London. But it took him a long while to make sure of his new path, and meanwhile he went on writing Italian operas for Vienna and Naples, and establishing his position with the public, and in the favour of the Viennese court and aristocracy. His first definite step in the new direction was "Orfeo ed Euridice" (libretto by Calzabigi), which came out in Vienna in 1762, and it was followed by "Alceste" in 1767, and "Paride ed Elena" in 1769. To the published edition of "Alceste" he added a preface explaining his views. He said he aimed at avoiding the "abuses which had crept into

Italian opera through the mistaken vanity of singers and the unwise compliance of composers"—that he endeavoured " to restrict music to its proper function, that of seconding the poetry by enforcing the expression of the sentiment "; that he " avoided making too great a disparity between the recitatives and the arias," and sought to make everything, including the overture and the orchestration, relevant and appropriate.

Though he succeeded fairly well in Vienna he was not satisfied that his reforms made sufficient effect there, and resolved to carry on his campaign in Paris, which seemed a more central position. On arriving there he began by putting his views forward vigorously in published letters, and by rousing public attention through notable literary men and public characters whom he interested in his scheme. And finally through the help of Marie Antoinette, whom he had taught singing in Vienna, he brought out, in 1774, a practical illustration of his theories in the shape of the music-drama " Iphigénie en Aulide," founded on the play by Racine. This was well received by the Parisians, and he followed up his success with revised versions of " Orfeo " and " Alceste " in 1776, and by the new opera of " Armide " in 1777. Meanwhile the opposition of the partisans of the old order grew more definite and determined. They adopted the Italian composer Piccini as their champion, and in a short time Paris was divided into the ardent factions called Piccinists and Gluckists.

Piccini was a much younger man than Gluck, having been born in 1728, but he was no unworthy rival. He had made notable successes in early years by light comic operas, of which the most successful was " La Cecchina," a work performed with phenomenal success all over Europe. He also produced successful specimens of the typical opera seria, and was with good reason considered the ablest living Italian composer. He had even attempted improvements and reforms on his own part, by more careful and intelligent use of the orchestra than usual, and by more suitable dramatic treatment of the ensembles. He was persuaded to come to Paris, and brought out, in 1778, his first French opera, " Roland," a setting of the same libretto used long before by Lulli. It was very successful, and the opposing factions seemed thereby fairly balanced. By way of bringing the contest to an effective issue it was proposed that both composers should set the same subject, " Iphigénie en

Tauride." Gluck's was ready first, and came out with great effect in 1779. Piccini's version was delayed by certain misadventures, and another of his operas, "Atys," was first produced with a success which it fully merited before his version of the test subject finally came out in 1781. It won a fair measure of success, but could not stand against the dramatic sincerity and striking character of Gluck's work, and the Gluckists were acknowledged to have the best of the contest. But Piccini's was an honourable defeat, and he was so far from being effaced by it that he continued to compose, and to be received with much favour in Paris and elsewhere; and the misfortunes of the latter part of his career were less owing to the result of the famous contest than to the general disturbances which followed the French Revolution. He died in 1800.

Gluck, on the other hand, practically ended his career with his victory. He wrote one light work for the French Court, called "Echo et Narcisse," and began another serious work called "Les Danaides," on his favourite classical lines; but his health broke down before he could finish it, and he handed it over to his pupil Salieri. He died in Vienna in 1787.

Gluck's position in musical history is very similar to Wagner's in recent times. His indictment against contemporary opera made much the same points as the modern composer's. But he laboured under the obvious disadvantage of living at a time when the development of resources, such as are characteristic of regular modern music, was yet slender. The arts of orchestration were only just beginning to be understood, and the arts of dramatic expression of the modern type were both limited in amount and but vague in general character, while the subtler possibilities of modulation were hardly thought of. Like Wagner he was not blessed with musical gifts of any very exceptional calibre to start with, but like his modern prototype he developed what he had with exceptional success under the influence of great dramatic and poetic sympathy and insight. His later work is unique in style and in the dignified sincerity with which he treats great and pathetic situations. Even when he had to compromise with popular taste, as in the excessive use of the ballet which was required by French audiences, he succeeded in making it tell as part of the dramatic effect. And the same may be said of his use of arias, which he dispensed with as much as possible in favour of a shorter and more concentrated form of solo, while he raised the recitative whenever possible to a high degree of dramatic interest.

A fact which marks his position well is that he is the earliest opera composer who can arouse the sympathies of a modern audience, in strong contrast to the utterly defunct formality of Hasse, Galuppi, Jomelli, and hundreds of other composers of that class.

Mozart's career as an opera composer overlaps .nat of Gluck; in fact, his earlier operas came out before the famous Parisian campaign; but it was not till after that episode that he produced the works by which he is remembered. His early operas only serve to illustrate the strength of the Italian influence to which he was subjected.

The European fame which Mozart attained when almost a child led to his having plenty of invitations to write operas. The earliest of any dimensions which was publicly performed was "La finta semplice," written for Vienna in 1768, when he was twelve. Owing to intrigues its first appearance was made in his native town Salzburg instead of Vienna. It was followed shortly after by "Mitridate," a full sized opera seria composed for Milan by invitation, and produced there in 1770 when he was fifteen. Its success led to further opportunities, and in the following year he produced "Il Sogno di Scipione" (1772), "Lucio Silla" (1772), "La finta Giardiniera" (1775), and "Il Re pastore" (1775). In these early years he could hardly have heard any operas which were not of the conventional Italian pattern, and indeed very little music of any kind which did not come from the southern source. This Italian influence was paramount through his lifetime, and illustrates the shifting of the highest level of musical composition from the vigorous North German Protestantism of Bach and Handel to the region in which Southern German gaiety and expansiveness adopted the Italian style and forms of music, and ultimately developed them to the very highest point which the art has ever attained. The completeness of this change is chiefly owing to Mozart's genius, but it was not till the flood of prosperity which attended his youth had given place to the troubles and crosses of the latter part of his short life that he produced works of sufficient mark to change the course of history.

The unfortunate visit to Paris in 1778 marks the turning-point of his career. On his way there he made a prolonged stay at Mannheim, and became intimate with the traditions of Stamitz and with a group of sincere and earnest-minded musicians, of whom Cannabich was foremost; and here he heard, possibly for the first time, really refined performances of orchestral music, which clearly made a great impression upon him.

He arrived in Paris just in the heat of the excitement about Gluck and Piccini, and though he stayed several months he never gained any notice, or any opportunity of distinguishing himself except by the production of his Parisian Symphony. This was by far the best he had yet written, but in Paris it did not bring him any particular repute, and, failing altogether to get a chance of producing an opera there, he returned to Salzburg in 1779.

His disappointments and troubles in Paris, where as a child he had been so wildly petted and caressed, may have had something to do with his being so little affected by the controversy about Piccini and Gluck. It is clear that Gluck's works made no great impression either upon his style or his methods of composition; but the trials of the journey and the change from the too easy success of his early years to the severe struggle of his maturity seem to have braced him to a higher standard of work. After a pause in opera writing for some years, he was invited to write an opera for the Carnival at Munich in 1781. For this occasion he wrote "Idomeneo," which is the first example of his more mature style. It is particularly noteworthy for the very rich and elastic treatment of the orchestra and for the effective choruses which are introduced. Its success bettered his position somewhat, and was followed by an invitation from the Austrian Emperor to write a genuine German opera.

The Emperor had long had it in mind to make an effort for the cause of National Opera, which had hitherto been in a very backward state. The vigorous efforts Keiser had made at Hamburg had collapsed with his death, and all Germany had been again occupied with Italian operas, frequently written by her own composers. The only German form which had a sustained popularity was that of the "Singspiel" or song play, a rather insignificant kind of work, consisting mainly of an ordinary theatrical piece interspersed liberally with songs and incidental music, like the English plays of Purcell's time and a little later. The most successful composers of such works (which were chiefly light and lively) were the following: Adam Hiller (1728—1804), who won considerable success with "Die verwandelten Weiber," a version of an English play, "The Devil to pay," and with "Der Dorfbarbier," "Die Jagd," and many others. Dittersdorf (1739—1799) was particularly successful in his "Doctor und Apotheker." Neefe (1748—1798), Beethoven's Master in Bonn, won success in the same lines, as did also Johann Schenck (1753—1836); and Kauer (1751—1831) is said to have written over 200 examples of this kind. It was for the development of a slender form of this sort into a type more worthy of being nationally representative that Mozart at the invitation of the Austrian Emperor produced his "Entführung aus dem Serail." It came out in 1782, and for once raised a Singspiel into the loftier region of first-rate art. It was the best work of its kind which Mozart had produced, and was too good for "Singspiel" audiences. The result was that Mozart received no encouragement to repeat the experiment for some time, and resumed the writing of Italian operas. The next which followed was the ever-fresh "Nozze di Figaro," which came out in 1786. It had the special advantage of being founded upon a first-rate French play, "Le Mariage de Figaro," by Beaumarchais, which was made up into a capital libretto by a clever Italian, Da Ponte. Its first performance at Vienna was not successful at all in proportion to its merits, but it was received with wild enthusiasm at Prague soon after. This success encouraged him to write another opera specially for Prague, and "Don Giovanni" (Da Ponte's libretto again) came out there in October, 1787. Its success on that occasion was worthy of the work, but when performed in Vienna later, it is said to have been only moderately successful; as the Viennese were persuaded by fair means or foul to prefer the "Tarare" of Salieri, Gluck's pupil, who is generally acknowledged to have carried on systematic intrigues against Mozart all through the latter part of his career. It is fortunate that a comparison between "Don Giovanni" and Salieri's works is no longer possible, except in the quiet seclusion of musical libraries. "Figaro" and "Don Giovanni" will always remain the representative examples of Mozart's Italian operas, and are utterly different from the works of his predecessors in every particular which gives musical and artistic value. Mozart was not by nature a reformer like Gluck, neither could he have expounded a systematic theory. His reforms were the direct fruit of

spontaneous genius and quickness of perception. In
"Figaro" and "Don Giovanni" the plays are no mere pegs
to hang pretty tunes on, but are amusing in themselves;
and Mozart's quickness has made the music reinforce every
point of the story, even to mere slight details of theatrical
business, which he seems to have had in his mind while
composing. The human interest in them is immensely
assisted by the element of comedy which Mozart illustrated
with unsurpassable skill in the style of the Italian opera
buffa and the intermezzi. In his hands instrumentation
rose for the first time to a condition of mature and complete
art. He was the first composer who had a refined feeling for
orchestral colour, and in opera he used this faculty with a
natural ease and readiness; while his general power and
mastery of his craft enabled him to develop ensembles and
finales to a degree of effectiveness and dramatic relevancy
which no previous composer had approached. Gluck surpassed him only in intensity in the situations which were
suitable to the peculiar cast of his poetic temperament.

The remainder of Mozart's Italian operas do not call for
much consideration. The opera buffa "Così fan tutte"
was written by order of the Emperor and performed in
Vienna in 1790; and the opera seria "Clemenza di Tito"
was written for a grand coronation ceremony in 1791. The
libretto of the latter was a hack subject with Italian composers, written by Metastasio, and first set by Caldara in 1734,
and used by Hasse, Gluck, Jomelli, and many others besides
Mozart.

Quite at the end of his career Mozart had one more
chance to make a stroke for German art, and the stroke was
lastingly effectual. Not long after the successful launch of
"Don Giovanni" he was applied to by Schikaneder—a
man who combined the gifts of actor, playwright, manager,
and man of enterprise—to set a fairy play which he had put
together, and believed would attract the genuinely German
masses. This was "Die Zauberflöte"; or, "The magic
Flute," a play which is certainly not easily intelligible to the
uninitiated, but contained enough mystery and magic and
opportunities for scenic display to attract a German
audience. Mozart set it to music in a manner which differs
to a considerable degree from all his earlier works, as
much of it is on a higher level. The peculiarity of the play
has hindered its popularity in other countries, but Schikaneder rightly gauged its fitness for a thorough German

audience, and the great success it ultimately won may fairly be said to be the definite starting-point of the successful development of the modern German music-drama, of which Weber, Beethoven, and Wagner are the foremost representatives.

Mozart was rapidly breaking down at the time of writing the "Zauberflöte," and he did not survive to witness the complete spread of its popularity, but died on December 5, 1791.

A few contemporaries of Mozart deserve record for creditable and occasionally brilliant work in the operatic line. Sarti (1729—1802, organist of Faenza, 1748) produced his first opera, "Pompeo in Armenia," there in 1751; his best opera is said to have been "Giulio Sabino." He met Mozart in Vienna in 1784, and spoke of him afterwards as a musical barbarian. Time has avenged the younger composer.

Paisiello (1741—1815) belonged to the school of Naples, where he was a pupil of Durante. His music was elegant and successful, and was specially admired by Napoleon. He wrote a "Barbiere di Siviglia," which was so popular that when Rossini endeavoured to get his setting performed the attempt was considered nothing less than presumption on his part and was at first vigorously hissed. Paisiello wrote in all ninety-four operas.

Sacchini (1734—1786) was also one of the Neapolitan school, and a pupil of Durante. He travelled to England and also to Paris, where he became very popular. His best operas were "Olimpiade," "Dardanus," "Œdipus," and "Tigrane."

The most brilliant member of this group was Cimarosa, born near Naples, 1749, and a member of the Neapolitan school. He early won reputation by his lively intermezzi. His first opera was "Le Stravaganze del Conte," 1772, his most famous was the "Matrimonio Segreto," one of the best and most brilliant opera buffas ever written. It came out first in Vienna in 1792, the year after Mozart died. His most successful serious opera was "Gli Orazii e Curiazii." He lived till 1801.

Salieri (1750—1825), Gluck's pupil, is most familiarly remembered for the reputation he won for scheming to prevent Mozart's success, but it may be remembered as a set-off that he acted to a certain extent as Schubert's master, and was held in some respect by Beethoven, who actually took lessons from him. He superintended most of the music of the Court and opera of Vienna, and wrote many successful operas.

The Belgian Grétry (1741—1813) also requires notice as a representative of the Parisian section of opera writers. He was a poor musician, but made success through a certain gift of tune and expression, and a delicate sense of humour. Born at Liége, he went to Rome for musical study, and became the despair of his master. But he was quite confident of himself, and in 1767 applied to Voltaire for a libretto, which was declined. He was the first representative composer of operas comiques, and wrote some fifty operas for Paris, of which "Le Huron" was the first (1768) and "Le tableau parlant," "Zemir et Azor," and "Richard" were the best.

Of Mozart's junior contemporaries, the most notable was Cherubini (1760—1842). He was brought up in the atmosphere of Italian music, but his disposition caused him to take a more serious view of the art than most of his fellow-countrymen, and this has given him a position which is quite unique among them. His views were so extremely severe that he appeared pedantic even to Mendelssohn; but, notwithstanding, his works have a genuine freshness and vitality. He began opera writing with "Quinto Fabio" in 1780. He came to England in 1784, and brought out some operas here, and finally settled in Paris in 1788. The first of his operas which won permanent fame was "Lodoiska," which came out in 1791. The light opera "Les deux journées" came out in 1800, and the famous "Medea" in 1797. These two represent extremes of different character, as the former is sparkling and bright and the latter a very severe tragedy. In both he succeeded equally well. His sense for dramatic effect was strong, but was always kept within bounds by a very sensitive taste, and his orchestration is often admirable. He was so much revered by musicians in Paris that in old age he was looked upon as a sort of autocratic censor.

Mehul (1763—1817) was a composer who held a great position in Paris about the same time. He was looked upon as the foremost French composer of the Revolution period. His best work, "Joseph," was his last, and came out in 1807. He had a genuine feeling for dramatic effect of a refined quality, and his orchestration was good.

Another composer of more striking calibre was Gasparo

Spontini. He was born at Majolati in 1774, and educated at Naples. His first opera, " I puntigli delle donne," was brought out in Rome in 1796. His early works are in the light Neapolitan style. He went to Paris in 1803, but did not make the mark he hoped for in the light style, and therefore changed his tactics completely for a style of the utmost grandioseness. " La Vestale " was finished in 1805, and first performed in 1807. The excellent libretto by Jouy was much in its favour, and the music is also remarkably fine. Spontini here displayed a great gift for rich orchestration, and a sense of broad and large effect, and a mastery of resource combined with a very considerable power of dramatic expression which give him a high place among composers. " La Vestale " thoroughly deserved the estimation in which it has since been held all over Europe. He followed it up by " Fernand Cortez," which is on much the same grandiose lines, in 1809. He was made conductor at the Italian Opera in Paris in 1810, and brought out Mozart's " Don Giovanni " for the first time in that city. His next large work was " Olympia," which occupied him many years, but did not succeed in Paris. When he went to Berlin to manage operatic affairs as Capellmeister and General Director of the music of the Court of King Frederick William, he remodelled it and brought it to a hearing there in 1821 with triumphant success. Unluckily for Spontini, Weber's "Der Freischütz" came out soon after in Berlin and took such hold of the hearts of Germans, with its thoroughly Teutonic flavour, that Spontini's supremacy was checked. He brought out several more operas, such as " Nurmahal " (1822), " Alcidor " (1825), " Agnes von Hohenstaufen " (1829), but by degrees he became very unpopular, partly owing to his autocratic disposition, and after a period of tension, in which he seems to have shown some force of character, he finally left Berlin in 1842 and returned to Italy, where he died in 1851. He was a commanding and conspicuous figure, and his works have grand and impressive qualities. They belong to the class of French grand opera, and stand midway between the statuesque beauty of Gluck and the meretricious pomp of Meyerbeer, who was his successor in Berlin.

CHAPTER IX.

THE PROGRESS OF INSTRUMENTAL MUSIC TO BEETHOVEN AND HIS IMMEDIATE SUCCESSORS.

WHILE Haydn and Mozart were applying their great powers to the advancement of the highest forms of instrumental music, some very valuable work was being done in various subordinate branches by other composers and performers, of considerable though less comprehensive powers. The prominent position taken by the pianoforte in modern music gives special importance to the work of Muzio Clementi, who was the first composer to show a clear perception of the style of performance required by that instrument as distinguished from the old harpsichord. Till he applied his mind to the subject composers had mainly kept to the quiet gliding style suitable to the older instrument, and hardly realised the effects and contrasts which were obtainable by the more forcible and energetic treatment which was invited by the use of hammers instead of jacks as a means of producing the sound. Clementi was born in Rome in 1752. He was solidly grounded in contrapuntal studies, and came before the public as a composer, with a mass, at the age of fourteen. He was brought to England by a rich amateur while still quite young, and made his first appearance in London in 1777; and with the exception of a few professional tours through Europe he remained in this country for the rest of his life. He was of a practical turn of mind, and, besides establishing a very good position as a teacher and a performer and a conductor at the opera, he founded a pianoforte business, which still exists as Messrs. Collard and Collard. He wrote a very large quantity of sonatas of very solid and artistic quality, but his best known work is the "Gradus ad Parnassum," a collection of his most excellent pianoforte studies, which he completed in 1817, when about sixty-five years old. He survived till 1832. The comprehensive quality and vigour of his work, and its perfect fitness for the pianoforte, justifies his being called the father of modern pianoforte music.

Among his pupils the most important was J. B. Cramer,

whose Studies hold so honourable a position among works of their class. They are more genial than Clementi's, though not so masculine. Cramer, like his master, was a thorough musician, and his insight into the requirements of the pianoforte is remarkably acute. He came of a family of musicians; and both his grandfather, as flute-player, and his father, as violinist, were members of the famous Mannheim band. He himself was born in Mannheim in 1771, but was brought to England by his father when one year old, and settled permanently in this country, where he also founded a music business, and held a distinguished position as a pianist and a teacher. He died in 1858.

Another famous pupil of Clementi was the Irishman, John Field (1782—1837), who was a very able pianist, and wrote a large quantity of pianoforte music, of which his nocturnes still enjoy the appreciation of musicians. He settled in St. Petersburg. Among those who did good service in developing the resources of the pianoforte was J. L. Dussek, born in Bohemia in 1761. He began his career as an organist, but ultimately became one of the greatest pianists of his time and enjoyed a European fame. He was for a short time a pupil of Philip Emmanuel Bach's, and wrote a large quantity of sonatas in a graceful and fluent style, which exerted no little influence upon some later composers for the instrument. He lived till 1812. His contemporary, Daniel Steibelt, had a considerable vogue as a player and composer and fashionable teacher in Paris and London successively. The date of his birth was 1755; he died 1823.

Among the prominent representatives of instrumental music of this intermediate stage, Ignaz Pleyel deserves mention. He was born in Austria in 1757, became one of Haydn's favourite pupils, and showed such good promise in early years as to have his quartets highly spoken of by Mozart. He wrote a large quantity of symphonies and chamber music, came to England for a time in 1791, simultaneously with Haydn's first visit with Salomon, and ultimately settled in Paris, where he founded a successful pianoforte factory. He died in 1831. Madame Pleyel, the famous pianist, was his daughter-in-law.

A composer who enjoyed a remarkable popularity for a time was A. Gyrowetz, born in Bohemia in 1763. He studied in Prague and then went to Vienna, where he received friendliness and encouragement from Mozart. His reputation was so good that he was engaged as a composer by Salomon at the same time with Haydn. He ultimately settled in Vienna and lived till 1850. So that having been born but a few years after Mozart, and having known him and Haydn intimately, he survived Mendelssohn and might have heard several of Wagner's operas. He also survived his own popularity. He wrote a large quantity of operas and cantatas and an immense number of symphonies and quartets. The symphonies are on a larger scale and more freely and intelligently scored than those of the previous generation, but they have not the distinction and artistic completeness of Haydn's and Mozart's, though they were sufficiently good for some of them to be passed off as Haydn's in Paris, till he went there and established his title to their authorship.

A family who did distinguished service to the cause of modern instrumental music were the Rombergs. Bernhard Romberg (1767—1841) was one of the earliest of great German cello players, and did a great deal to advance the technique of that instrument. He wrote quartets and a number of cello concertos, which are so admirably suited for the instrument as to be still valuable for teaching purposes. His cousin, Andreas Romberg, was a famous violinist and composer (1767—1821). He began his successful career as a player at the age of seven, and produced in the course of his life a great variety of compositions, such as operas, cantatas, symphonies, and quartets, which had wide popularity and no inconsiderable merit.

The greatest representative of pure instrumental music, Louis van Beethoven, was born in 1770, at Bonn, where his father was a tenor singer in the chapel of the Elector of Cologne. His youth had none of the opportunities nor the brilliancy of Mozart's, and he developed slowly, in circumstances which forced him to get such musical education as he could by his own exertions. He had for masters the organists of the Chapel, van den Eeden, and Neefe, and he early occupied the position of accompanist at the local theatre. He also learnt the viola and played in the band. The music performed during his youth was not of the highest class, though of fair average merit of the time; such as works of Sarti, Salieri, and Paisiello. He went to Vienna for a short time in 1787, where he met Mozart, who was struck by his extemporising. Haydn passed through Bonn in 1790 and 1792 on his way to England and back, and on the second occasion Beethoven showed him a cantata, which Haydn seemed to think well of His powers were by this time becoming sufficiently noticeable for the Elector to send him to Vienna to study under Haydn, and he went there in 1792, when he was already twenty-one, and still had a great deal of his education to accomplish. His work with Haydn was no great success, for the old master was too busy to attend to him, and they were not altogether congenial in disposition. So when Haydn started for England in 1794 Beethoven transferred himself to the well-known theorist Albrechtsberger. With him he worked energetically at counterpoint, fugue, and canon, with the result that his master declared him to be a very unsatisfactory and unpromising pupil. His relations with his fellow musicians were not very friendly, for he thought poorly of most of them and did not disguise his opinion. But he won many ardent friends amongst aristocratic amateurs; and in the year 1795 he practically made his first public entry on his career by playing one of his earliest concertos at a public concert, and publishing the first of his works which have an "opus" number. These were the three Trios, Opus 1, and the three Sonatas (dedicated to Haydn), Opus 2; and from that point his mature years may be said to begin, and the details of his life have thenceforward only a secondary importance. The opportunities of his youth had been singularly meagre. He could have heard but very little choral music of good quality, and though his experiences were more rich in the line of operatic music, he could have heard very few operas that were better than second rate till he was nearly twenty; and his knowledge of orchestral works was equally limited, both through his living at Bonn and by the obvious fact that hardly any first rate and mature symphonies existed before the year 1786. His musical education was also to all appearances very backward, but that may possibly have been a minor drawback, as he was forced to develop his own powers and find out his own way in art, and was thereby strengthened in individuality and character.

The most obvious feature of his compositions as a whole is the immense preponderance of works in the form of sonatas. At the beginning of his career he published thirty consecutive works, every one of which is in sonata form; and in the whole list of his works—including masses, songs, variations, fugues, cantatas, and an opera—more than one-half are of the same order. The explanation lies in the fact that the artistic progress of music for nearly two hundred years had centred round the development of harmonic form, of which the sonata is the finest type; and Beethoven, as the man most highly gifted in his time, and with the keenest feeling for design and expression, naturally adopted the form which afforded him the richest opportunities; and circumstances being in every way favourable, he carried the treatment of the sonata to the highest perfection of which that form of art seems capable. He infused into it a new element of meaning and expression, without losing hold of the perfect balance of the design, and he immensely enriched and widened the scope of art in all directions to make room for the force and variety of his ideas; so that in the end the lover of strong impressions finds all he longs for, while the worshipper of abstract perfection in art rests satisfied that Beethoven was essentially a master of form.

In his early period, up to Opus 50, the influence of the style of the previous generation is more obviously apparent. This period, lasting till about his thirty-third year, comprises his first two Symphonies in C and D, three concertos, the well-known septet, and a number of fine sonatas, such as that in C sharp minor, Opus 27, that in A flat with the variations, the remarkably rich and interesting one in D minor, and the superb " Kreutzer " Sonata for pianoforte and violin. In some few of these, such especially as the last two, he gives a foretaste of his finest qualities; a variety and a scope, and a power for manipulating his design which no man ever showed before. After Opus 50 he passed into a new and more emotional and vigorous manner—the style of his best and happiest years. The mass of his best-known and best-loved works succeeded each other in rapid succession: The "Waldstein" Sonata (Opus 53), the "Appassionata" (Opus 57), his third Symphony called "Eroica" (Opus 55), the Concerto in G major (Opus 58), the "Rasoumoffsky" Quartets (Opus 59), the fourth Symphony in B flat (Opus 60), the Violin Concerto (Opus 61), the Overture to "Coriolan" (Opus 62), the C minor Symphony (Opus 67) (which constantly maintains its position as the favourite of all his orchestral works), the "Pastoral" Symphony (Opus 68), the Sonata in A for pianoforte and cello (Opus 69), the two Pianoforte Trios (Opus 70), his one opera "Fidelio" (Opus 72), the famous Concerto in E flat (Opus 73), and many other splendid and notable works. These represent the most important of his works up to almost the year 1810, when he was nearly forty years old. Meanwhile he had been gradually passing under the influence of the two greatest trials of his life, which permanently affected his moods and character. The first and most obvious was his deafness. This began to afflict him ominously as early as 1798, when he was but twenty-eight; by 1814 it had grown so serious that he had to give up performing in public and conducting rehearsals and all work which depended much on certainty of hearing; by 1816 he had to resort to an ear-trumpet, and soon after that he ceased to hear so completely that all communications with other people had to be carried on in writing, and only on rare occasions was anything ever audible to him again. Another trouble was owing to a nephew whose father had died, and whom Beethoven wished to take into sole guardianship. This brought upon him unlimited trouble, lawsuits, and vexations; his work was for a time seriously interfered with, and contingent worries caused him to become more morose and isolated than ever. His deafness reacted upon his art and more than ever intensified his originality and depth of thought, while his other troubles intensified his earnestness and style of utterance. To these two influences may be chiefly attributed the final change of his style, which began to be apparent soon after Opus 90 in such works as his E minor Sonata (Opus 91) and his F minor Quartet, and found its highest expression in the last five sonatas, the last quartets from Opus 127 onwards, the great Mass in D, and the final and greatest triumph of his life, the Choral Symphony (Opus 125).

Beethoven was impelled to widen out and enrich his scheme in every respect. His thorough appreciation of the pianoforte, with its new opportunities of effect and richness of sound, and the important adjunct of the pedal, made him adopt, in writing for that instrument, a much more powerful style, and aim at effects which had a far greater volume of tone than had ever been attempted or thought of before; while his instinct for harmonic variety and the effects which are obtainable by new and striking progressions and subtle use of modulation gave him the highest power of expression the art is capable of. In his symphonies he adopted from the first a larger group of instruments than his predecessors—invariably including clarinets with hautboys as an additional element of colour—and he soon found out how to use the various instruments, wind, strings, and drums, with more genuine independence, and with more real sense of their respective characteristics, and a more perfect blending into one complete whole than his predecessors had done. In grouping his movements, too, he soon became more free than they had been. At first he adopted a scheme of four movements, but soon found that much was to be gained by varying their order, number, and character. So that in some of his finest sonatas he adopted a group of three movements, or even sometimes only two, as better adapted to give individual character to the complete work; and sometimes he extended the scheme to five movements, as in the Pastoral Symphony. But he set his impress equally upon all the movements. His first Allegros became more definite in character, and more closely knit by the use of short incisive figures instead of long melodious subjects; his slow movements passed out of the phase of being like the old opera arias into the most romantic and impassioned forms, full of human feeling and even dramatic effect. His last movements grew more serious and solid and dignified than had been usual with earlier composers, while in changing the minuet movement (which had represented the dance type in a graceful and uniform manner) into the Scherzo, he gave to art one of the most vivid, characteristic, and effective of all modern art forms—one eminently calculated to express his sense of humour, fun, wit, irony, and subtlety of thought; and at the same time supplying a much more complete counterpoise to the sentiment of the slow movement than had before existed in the group of sonata movements. The slow introductory movements he sometimes adopted were quite a new departure in art. Previous to his time such movements had been extremely limited in range of harmony, and very formal in character. He entirely transformed them by introducing remarkable modulations, and by interesting ideas and devices of form; and sometimes developed them to such a pitch of importance that the Introductions to the "Kreutzer" Sonata, to the Symphonies in B flat and A, and to the Overture to "Leonore" are among the most wonderful of his achievements. In the internal organisation of the movements a like power of expansion is shown in the wonderful episodes, and the unexpected digressions (which are always perfectly coherent to the design), and the novelty and interest and wide range of his *Codas*.

His tendency towards direct and decided expression is

marked by his frequent adoption of a recognisable purpose in composing his works, as illustrated most remarkably in the "Eroica" Symphony—which was written in honour of Napoleon Bonaparte before he became Emperor—in the "Pastoral" Symphony, and in the two sonatas which bear distinct names. In the C minor Symphony and the seventh in A an equally strong impression of something behind the music is apparent, and in all these respects he became the first notable exponent of the modern tendency towards what is sometimes called programme—which really means illustrating by music some definite conception, or circumstances which have a poetic or dramatic import external to the music itself. But with him the work never depends upon the programme for its effect, and he is careful to avoid attempting to paint scenes in musical figures; and some of those movements which are most obviously founded on an idea external to music are specially perfect and beautiful in form. He understood art too well by instinct to be misled into thinking that mere force, or vehemence, or definiteness of expression can make good works of art; and the greatness of his effects consists even more in the perfect management of the relative parts of his entire works, and their bearing upon one another, than in the mere ideas themselves.

His methods of composition were also very different from those of his predecessors, except J. S. Bach, for he re-wrote and remodelled everything over and over again. Even his ideas were recast and reconsidered many times over before he was satisfied with them, and the contents of his numerous sketch-books bear eloquent testimony to his patience and self-criticism. His methods of work were much more like those of *littérateurs*, poets, painters, and sculptors than those usual with musical composers, and his works accordingly bear the marks of a higher degree of concentration and a wider range of expression and design; and the sum of the result is the richest and most perfect form of abstract instrumental art which exists in the whole range of music.

Contemporary with Beethoven, but representing an earlier state of art in many ways, was Johann Nepomuk Hummel (1778—1837). He had the great advantage of not only being Mozart's pupil, but of living for two years in his house. In his prime he was considered the most brilliant of German pianists, and had a very high reputation as a composer. He had a great talent for the ornamental part of music, and produced many large works which have a certain elegance and finish, but comparatively little substance. He exercised considerable influence upon many composers for the pianoforte in the succeeding generations, including Chopin.

The composers who came after Beethoven tended more and more to aim at direct expression of ideas external to music, but they immediately began to lose hold of full mastery and control of design. This is strongly noticeable even among his junior contemporaries.

Carl Maria von Weber is chiefly important through the position he occupies as the first representative of true German national opera, in spirit and in method; but his instrumental music also has a position of some importance in history. He was born in 1786, sixteen years after Beethoven. He came of somewhat different stock from most of the earlier composers, having some claims to aristocratic blood. His musical education was very imperfect, as his father was anxious to push him into notice too early, and without any real solid grounding. But he had great gifts, considerable sense of effect, and a highly strung and imaginative temperament. His sonatas illustrate the tendencies of modern instrumental music, by the skilful use of pianoforte effect, the dependence upon showy qualities in the performer, and the predominance of sentiment over closeness and concentration of design. In such things Weber shows the insight of the performer rather than the musician, of the elocutionist rather than the genuine orator; but his methods and treatment of the instrument undoubtedly impressed very distinguished composers in later times, and his influence upon art in that respect cannot be gainsaid. His impulse for adopting a definite external idea is most strongly emphasized in his Concertstück for pianoforte and orchestra, written in 1821, which was avowedly written to illustrate a fanciful episode about a knight and a lady in the days of the Crusades. His genius shone at its brightest in the management of orchestral effect, as illustrated most happily in his famous Overtures to "Der Freischütz," "Oberon," and "Euryanthe." In his use of the characteristic qualities of tone of different instruments to illustrate special dramatic or poetic ideas he is one of the foremost of modern composers. He specially delights in things weird and magical—the music of the "Wolf's Glen," the magic music of fairies. In these things he expresses a trait of the Teutonic disposition, and also shows strongly the influence of the theatre. Here again it is perceptible that the influence which raises him to his best achievement is a conception external to music, and not the spontaneous musical impulse such as commonly impelled composers before Beethoven's time. Weber's career was a short one; his delicate constitution was early worn out by the strain put upon it from the first, and he died in London in June, 1826, when he was over here to superintend the first performance of his " Oberon."

Schubert's position in the history of art is centred mainly upon his songs; but his position as a writer of instrumental music is by no means insignificant. His opportunities in youth were even less favourable than Weber's. He was born of a poor schoolmaster's family, in January, 1797, in Vienna. He sang in the Imperial choir as a boy, and was sent to the school—called the Konvict—in which the members of the choir were educated. Here he heard a certain amount of music of various kinds—second-rate symphonies, masses, &c.—and spontaneously took to composing himself. His natural impulse was to look for external inspiration in poems, and under such influence he was at his best, and produced magnificent songs in quite early years. His models in instrumental music were not of the best, and his early efforts in the line of symphonies are comparatively tame; but as his experience of music enlarged, he found the way to express his ideas more completely in instrumental form. He was always uncertain in the management and control of design, but ideas of every kind were always ready in profusion, and take the hearer with them by qualities which are more direct and more in consonance with modern spirit than such purely artistic considerations as beauty and balance of design. Of all great composers he is the one who depends most on the actual attractiveness of his musical ideas and his musical personality; and these qualities have exercised great influence upon many composers of high rank in later times. The charm lies far more in his spontaneity than in his power of development or mastery of form. Judged from the abstract point of view as absolute music, his works of the sonata order are often obviously redundant and imperfect in design and bear cutting without much injury. Schubert in his profusion attacked all branches of instrumental music, and the best of his works of this kind belong to his later years, when his experiences had been enriched by hearing more first-rate music, such as some of Beethoven's most inspiring works. He set his seal upon this branch of art especially by his last two symphonic works—the delightful fragment known as the "Unfinished" Symphony in B minor and the grand Symphony in C major. These are the first orchestral works on a large scale in which his genuine characteristic musical nature shows itself, not only in the ideas and the manner of treatment, but even in the scoring—which is quite modern in its effect. The B minor fragment was written in 1822, and, therefore, preceded Beethoven's Ninth Symphony, while the C major Symphony was written in 1828, after the appearance of that immense work; and the influence of Beethoven here appears most strongly, both in the vigorous and full treatment of a large orchestra, in the characteristic *Scherzo*, and in the romantic tendency of almost every movement. Of his other instrumental works the most impressive are the "Rosamunde" Entr'actes, the Quartets in D minor and G, the Quintet in C, the Octet, the Pianoforte Trio in B flat, and some of the sonatas. But it is also noticeable, as a sign of the times, that among the most permanently interesting are works which are definitely outside the circle of sonatas, such as the great Fantasia in C, and some of the small impromptus and "Moments Musicaux." Schubert's life was cut short at thirty-one, in November, 1828, only one year after Beethoven.

Louis Spohr, owing to the length of his career, and the late date of the appearance of his most important works, seems to belong to a later generation than Weber and Schubert, though in reality he was born before either of them, in 1784. Seesen, in Brunswick, was his native place, where his father was a physician. He showed his powers as a violinist very early, and, combining natural aptitude with singular perseverance, he rightfully won the reputation of being the greatest German violinist before he had long passed the years of his youth. His first opportunity to bring out a large composition was at a festival in the little Thuringian town of Frankenhausen, in 1811, for which he wrote his first Symphony in E flat; and this was soon followed by oratorios and other important works, among them some of his best violin concertos. People soon learnt to regard him as one of the principal representative composers of the day, and his works comprise examples of every form of composition—operas, oratorios, cantatas, concertos, quartets, and symphonies. He wrote effectively, though not always judiciously, for the voice, but his chief importance lies in his connection with violin music and orchestral music, and among his firmest titles to fame is his invaluable Violin School, which came out in 1831.

In the matter of style he was quite out of sympathy with Beethoven, adopting a chromatic and sentimental manner which is curiously at variance both with his own personal character and the best spirit of his age. But his impulse was as much to seek inspiration and motive external to purely musical considerations as Beethoven, and he had a very predominant taste for new experiments. The most famous of his symphonies is called the "Weihe der Töne," known in this country as the "Power of Sound." It had been his intention to set a poem by Pfeiffer of that name, but finding that his setting did not satisfy him, he turned the work into a symphony, and directed that the poem should be read whenever it was performed. The earlier part of the work is on the usual symphonic lines, but the latter part, which is the weakest, comprises a march and two movements containing hymn tunes, and other points which depend on programme rather than genuine artistic excellence for their effect. This work came out in 1832, when Beethoven, Weber, and Schubert were all gone from the world. An extremely eccentric experiment in this line was his Historical Symphony, each movement of which was meant to represent a different period in the history of art. The first was meant to be in the style of Handel and Bach, the second in that of Mozart and Haydn, the third in that of Beethoven, and the last in the style of Spohr's day. His next symphony was equally curious, being descriptive of "The worldly and the divine in human life," for which two orchestras were employed—the usual full orchestra to express the worldly influences and an orchestra of solo instruments the heavenly ones. His Ninth Symphony, which was also his last, was called "The Seasons," and aimed at depicting the characteristics of the four principal divisions of the year. This came out in 1849, not only twenty years after the death of Beethoven, but even after that of Mendelssohn. It was almost his last instrumental composition on a large scale, though he lived on till October, 1859. His labours have a very wide range, including operas such as "Jessonda" (1822) and "Faust" (1818); oratorios, such as "The Last Judgment" (1826) and "The Fall of Babylon" (1842); but he is historically most important in matters connected with the violin and the orchestra. The perfection of his instinct for his own instrument places his compositions for it at the head of all modern works in respect of fitness and technique, especially in his numerous concertos; while his skilful orchestration marks a distinct advance in the use of variety of colour and effect of a modern kind. The influence of Mozart is more apparent than that of any other master, but his sentiment and his use of varieties of colour for distinct ends are essentially modern. He was a man of strong character, and his reputation in his lifetime was extraordinarily high; but his style was too deficient in genuine breadth and nobility to exert much permanent influence on his successors.

CHAPTER X.

MODERN INSTRUMENTAL MUSIC.

THE most notable composers who were born in the early years of the nineteenth century illustrate in a marked manner the general tendencies of artistic progress in instrumental music since Beethoven. Hector Berlioz, born 1803; Mendelssohn, 1809; Chopin, 1809; Schumann, 1810; Liszt, 1811; Henselt, 1814; Stephen Heller, 1815; Raff, 1822; Rubinstein, 1830, all show a disposition to drop the sonata form, and to seek new principles of procedure and greater variety of design to meet the requirement of new types of musical ideas, and new ways of looking at music.

The works of the first member of this group seem to emphasize most forcibly the tendencies towards "programme" and independence of form. But it must not be forgotten that the French have never shown any aptitude for pure instrumental music, and need the stimulus of ideas external to music to excite them to musical utterance. The stage is their natural field of artistic action, and the only music they have succeeded in at all notably is in some way connected with it, either as actual operas or as ballet tunes. The fact that Berlioz wrote large instrumental works on theatrical lines is, therefore, less significant historically than the fact that a programme was so frequently adopted by Teutonic composers. All the traditions of classical art were distasteful to his eager and impatient temperament. He regarded them as superfluous, and sought to employ music of the largest calibre with the most profuse resources of the orchestra to express stories and human circumstances which struck him as likely to be effective and interesting in a musical dress; and he hoped to attain, by following the working and sequence of the extra-musical ideas, an orderliness and aspect of design which should satisfy the mind as well as the classical types of form and development which he gladly dispensed with. His gifts were strongest in the direction of rhythm and colour. His excitable disposition was particularly susceptible to the qualities of tone of instruments, and he set himself deliberately to develop remarkable effects of instrumentation, and succeeded so well that it has given him a unique place among the foremost representatives of modern art. The masters he worshipped were Beethoven—for the force of his expression—and Gluck—for his dramatic power and insight. He was also under the influence of Spontini to some extent, and, in a lesser degree, of Mozart. But he was more influenced by the style of their utterances than by their artistic principles. He always depended upon the stimulus of a strong programme for his guide in action. His earliest instrumental works of mark were the Overtures to "Waverley," "Les Francs Juges," and "King Lear," all very characteristic and forcible productions. The larger instrumental works which represent him fully are the Symphonie fantastique called "Episode de la vie d'un artiste" (a thoroughly Parisian artist's fancy, ending with the guillotine and a mock Dies Iræ) and its sequel, "Lelio on le retour à la vie," *Monodrame lyrique.* "Harold en Italie," which he called a symphony, was written at the suggestion of Paganini, with a solo part, of no great prominence, for the viola. In these Berlioz only indicated a programme without setting words to be sung. His theories bore happiest fruit when the programme was helped out by soli and choruses, as in his "Damnation de Faust," which he called a *Legende dramatique.* His "Romeo et Juliette," which he called a dramatic symphony, contained some of his most remarkable instrumental experiments as well as vocal music. His principles of treatment are much the same in all these cases, as they are also in his sacred music, such as the "Grande Messe des Morts," the "Te Deum" and "L'Enfance du Christ," and also in his operatic works, "Benvenuto Cellini," "Beatrice et Benedict," and "Les Troyens." Like so many modern musicians of mark, he had considerable literary gifts, and supported himself mainly by writing for newspapers. Though the most remarkable composer France ever produced he was, in his own time, better appreciated in other countries than his own.

Though Mendelssohn's instrumental works are much less conspicuously of the programme order, his position as an essentially classical composer intensifies the inferences which his attitude in instrumental music suggests. Of all his numerous and popular solo works for the pianoforte and organ, hardly one belongs essentially to the sonata order.

He infused new life into the elastic and perennial forms of prelude and fugue, both for organ and pianoforte, and he produced one admirable example of the Variations form in the "Variations Sérieuses" (1841). He was conspicuously successful in what he called "Songs without words," which are short characteristic pieces in various forms, written at different times in his life from 1830 till the end. He was equally successful in organ works, and it is specially significant that most of those which are called sonatas are so only in name, and rarely have anything of the typical sonata character or principle of design about them. He was less successful in his capriccios and fantasias for the pianoforte, for in them his taste for brilliancy is shown at the expense of the musical material. The same gifts of brilliancy are applied, with much more happy results, in his Concertos for pianoforte and orchestra in G minor (1831) and D minor (1837), and in the Concerto for violin and orchestra (1844), which is one of the very finest of all his works. In pure orchestral music he appears at his best in the music for the "Midsummer Night's Dream." The admirable Overture to this was written when he was quite young (1826), and the remainder of the music was added at the request of the King of Prussia in 1843. Though comprising a certain quantity of vocal music, the most important parts of this work are the instrumental movements, such as the Overture, Scherzo, and Notturno, which are among the most characteristically effective of modern orchestral works.

For all his most successful symphonies he adopted distinctive names. He wrote a great number in youth which have not survived. Only the thirteenth, in C minor, is occasionally played. The earliest which has maintained any hold on the musical world is the "Reformation" Symphony, which was written for a great Protestant Tercentenary Festival at Augsburg in 1830. In this he endeavoured to carry out something of a programme by the use of such features as the famous formula for the "Amen," used at the Roman Church in Dresden, and familiar to musical audiences in later days by its use in Wagner's "Parsifal"; and also by the use of the famous chorale of Luther, "Ein feste Burg." His second Symphony, the "Italian," followed soon after, in 1833, and is a sort of subjective record of his happy impressions during a stay in Italy in 1830 and 1831. The next Symphony in order of time was the "Hymn of Praise," which was written for the Gutenberg Centenary Festival, held at Leipzig in 1840, to celebrate the invention of printing four hundred years before. It is on the same plan as Beethoven's Ninth Symphony, having the three instrumental movements of the usual type to begin with, and a series of choruses and solos to take the place of the last movement. It is happily unified by the recurrence of certain strongly characteristic phrases in various parts of the work; such as the opening phrase which is given out by the trombone. The next of Mendelssohn's Symphonies was the "Scotch," which came out in 1842, and stood in the same relation to the composer's experiences in Scotland as his "Italian" Symphony did to his visit to that country. And yet another most successful work which illustrates the same experiences is one of the best of his overtures, that known as "The Hebrides," or "Fingal's Höhle," 1830. In all these the tendency is observable to make the musical expression represent some definite thought which is external to the mere music. Mendelssohn was a classicist by nature, but even he fell in with the tendencies of his time; and though he was too wise to think weakness of design could be compensated for by programme or obviousness of meaning, he nevertheless in these most important cases allowed his inspiration to be impelled and nourished by a definite purpose.

The branch of chamber music is the one in which the traditions of the Sonata persist most conspicuously. In combinations of pianoforte with other solo instruments, composers seem to find opportunities to do something new in that form which are less attainable in other branches of art. Mendelssohn was very successful in that line, and his Trios for pianoforte and strings in C minor and D minor are among the most universally popular of all works of that class. His Quartets, Quintets, and Octet for strings, though sometimes rather orchestral in style, are also favourite examples of that refined class of art. His brilliant successes in other branches of art must be referred to elsewhere. He died in 1847.

Chopin was born less than a month after Mendelssohn. It illustrates the branching out of music into many different forms and styles that men so pre-eminent in art and yet so different in musical character should have been born so near together. Chopin is one of the most conspicuous representatives of the most modern type of music, for he is thoroughly independent of the conventions of classicism in art; but he is so far from being inartistic on that account, that the perfection of delicacy with which he applies all the richest resources of technique to the expression of his thoughts is almost without parallel. Moreover, though so specially notable as a master of the technique of performance, he really has musical thoughts which are worth expressing, and a genuine musical personality; and even the ornamental parts of his work—which form so important a feature in the stock-in-trade of virtuosi—in his case generally have real musical significance and beauty.

A great deal of the individuality of Chopin's music comes from the race to which he belonged and his early surroundings. His native country, Poland, had a long tradition of misfortune to look back upon; and nations in such circumstances commonly relieve their feelings in poetry and pathetic song. It appears to intensify the instinct for things imaginative, as well as racial characteristics. Chopin, who was born near Warsaw, imbibed the spirit of the Polish national music and dancing from early years, though their influence did not bear full fruit till experience had matured his powers. He began his career as a pianist, and before he was twenty had almost surpassed all rivals. He journeyed to Vienna and other musical centres giving concerts, and finally settled in Paris in 1831, just at the time when that city was fermenting with romanticism in literature and art. His compositions up to that time had comprised the set of Studies, Opus 10, which are undoubtedly the finest examples of their kind ever written for any instrument, and some of the Preludes, which are among the most interesting and poetical of his works. He had also written two concertos for his own use and a few movements representing or reflecting the style of the national dance music. But the mass of his mature and completely characteristic music was produced after he settled in Paris. Closer contact with musicians of high attainments, opportunities of hearing more music, and the romantic and intellectual ardour of the time widened his horizon and raised his standard, and he rapidly enriched the art with his great chivalric Polonaises, the romantic Ballades, the poetical Nocturnes, the brilliant Scherzos, the interesting and original Sonatas, and many other types of very characteristic art. He uttered his thoughts with complete certainty only through the medium of the pianoforte. He never became master of orchestration even sufficiently to write the accompaniments to his concertos with due effect. But his work for the pianoforte is so marvellously perfect in its adaptation to the idiosyncracies of the instrument, that it becomes historically important on that ground alone. His work is not often great in conception, or noteworthy in design, but it is the spontaneous expression of a poetical, refined, and sensitive temperament, and his style has exercised an almost universal influence upon writers of pianoforte music since his time, except in the case of a few specially strong-natured composers. Chopin made Paris his home and but rarely left it. He did not play much in public, but confined himself mainly to fashionable salons. He twice visited England, and twice Leipzig and Dresden, and other North German musical centres. One of the most important episodes in his life was his journey to Majorca with George Sand, the famous novelist, for his health. His vitality was broken early by the stress his excitable temperament put upon it, and he died in Paris in 1849.

The very next year after Chopin, Robert Schumann was born at Zwickau, in Saxony. He represents a phase of music as characteristically modern as Chopin's, but of different quality. The points where the two composers touch is in the romantic and poetical character of their ideas, the warmth of colour and richness of tone, and the strongly marked diversity of method from the old sonata type. They differ in depth of feeling and intellectuality. Chopin is at once lighter and more quickly sensitive—combining the poetry of the Pole with the alertness of a Parisian. Schumann is more reflective and intellectual, and saturated with Teutonic earnestness. Schumann indeed was the higher type of man, of purer aims, though of less brilliant skill. He was not intended for a musician, but for a lawyer, and was brought up from youth in constant contact with books; as his father was a bookseller, and also, in a moderate way, a literary man himself. Schumann fell under the influence of the romantic movement in German literature—especially under the spell of Jean Paul Richter—and he transmitted the figurative and metaphorical methods of this literature to his music. He aimed first at the career of a pianist, and studied with Wieck for some time—whose daughter, in later days, is known to all the world under Schumann's own name as one of the most ideal of living pianists. A permanent injury to a finger caused him to lay aside his aspirations to become a virtuoso and to devote himself to composition and to criticism. He and some friends of kindred spirit started a musical paper, Die neue Zeitschrift für Musik, in 1834; and for this Schumann wrote a remarkable series of articles on musical events and subjects; welcoming cordially, and with wonderful liberality and breadth of sympathy, every new worker in the field who had genuine musical disposition, of almost every school and style.

Schumann's own work was divided into a series of definite periods, as had been the case with Bach. He devoted himself at first mainly to writing sets of short and vivid pianoforte pieces, of wonderful variety of character and form: such as the Papillons (Op. 2), Intermezzi (Op. 4), Davidsbündlertänze (Op. 6), Carnaval (Op. 9), Fantasiestücke (Op. 12), Kinderscenen (Op. 15), Kreisleriana (Op. 16), Arabesque (Op. 18), Novelletten (Op. 21). With these were interspersed a few works on a larger scale, such as the Toccata (Op. 7), the Allegro (Op. 8), the Etudes Symphoniques (Op. 12), and the very remarkable and original Fantasia in C (Op. 17), the Faschingsschwank aus Wien, and three so-called sonatas, only one of which is at all like the old classical sonatas either in style or design. In all lines he endeavoured to find new and more elastic methods of applying musical art to the purposes of expression; and most of his pieces have definite names and special meanings, which are sometimes indicated by a verse of poetry. In the year 1840 he devoted himself mainly to song writing. That was the year of his marriage with Clara Wieck. In the following year he wrote several symphonic works. The first which can be said maturely to represent him is that in B flat. It is the one of all his works which is most nearly on classical lines. In the second he tried experiments in new lines, and endeavoured to unify the whole work by using characteristic figures throughout. It was originally called Symphonistische Phantasie, and was subjected to much alteration before it was finally published as Symphony No. 4, in 1851. Another important orchestral work of the year 1841 was the "Overture, Scherzo and Finale," which was originally intended to be a Sinfonietta. Part of the famous Pianoforte Concerto in A minor was also written at this time, but it was not completed till 1845. In the year 1842 he occupied himself mainly with chamber music, and produced two of his most popular works—the Pianoforte Quintet and the Quartet in E flat, besides string quartets and other examples of the same order of art. In later years he addressed himself to choral music and completed the series of his great instrumental compositions with the fine Symphony in C major (1845—1846) and the one in E flat, known as the "Rhenish" (1850), and the music to "Manfred," the overture to which is one of his finest and most complete orchestral works. But fine and noble in spirit as these are, he set his seal most effectually upon works in which the pianoforte takes the most prominent position; and especially in those in which he endeavoured to develop a new scheme or method of artistic procedure, and to use music as a vehicle for poetical thought. Much of the music of his later years suffers from the gradual increase of disease in the brain, of which he died in 1854.

It would be hard to find a more conspicuous contrast to Schumann than Franz Liszt, who came into the world but a year after him. He is mainly important in musical history as the representative of the most advanced standard of pianoforte technique, and the most brilliant virtuoso of his instrument who ever lived. He, as it were, summed up the labours of all previous players and inventors of devices of performance, and crowned them by his own special gift for contriving new and yet more brilliant effects. In his original compositions he was noteworthy as a prominent representative of radical theories for devising new principles of design and development; abandoning deliberately the classical principles of form, and trying to make movements intelligible by employing characteristic figures in a manner like the use of *Leitmotiven* by Wagner in music-dramas. His most important contributions to art in the line of programme music are the "Faust" and "Dante" Symphonies and the thirteen Symphonic Poems, which are specially remarkable on the score of orchestral effect; for his sense in that direction is of a kindred nature to his instinct for pianoforte effect. His pianoforte concertos also are remarkable for their brilliancy and novelty of treatment, and so are his pianoforte studies. A great proportion of his works are transcriptions of songs, opera airs, and national tunes, but even these are noteworthy for the truly extraordinary and intricate skill with which the resources of the instrument are applied.

Liszt was born at Raiding in Hungary. He played in public for the first time at Vienna in 1823, where he also had lessons from Czerny. He went to Paris in that same year, and from that time till about 1839 made that city his home.

Later he spent many years mainly in concert tours all over Europe. One of the most honourable episodes in his life was the period of twelve years previous to 1859 when he was conductor at Weimar, and brought out "Lohengrin," "Tannhäuser," "The Flying Dutchman," Berlioz's "Benvenuto Cellini," Schumann's "Genoveva," Schubert's "Alfonso and Estrella," and many other important works whose difficulties and high merits prevented less able and courageous conductors from attempting them. He became closely connected with Wagner, who married his daughter in 1870. He died at Bayreuth in 1886.

In the same year with Liszt was born Ferdinand Hiller, who was an efficient pianist, and a successful writer of pianoforte music, symphonies, and other kinds of music, of artistic but not very characteristic quality. He was a great friend of Mendelssohn's, but long survived him. He died in 1885.

As the pianoforte has become the familiar domestic instrument of the whole world it is natural that composers who aim at supplying music for it should spring up in legions. But not many have impressed sufficient individuality into their works to make them of any real historic importance. Among famous players of modern times Sigismund Thalberg takes high rank; in his time he was thought worthy of being compared with Liszt himself. He was a year younger than that master, being born in Vienna in 1812. He had an inventive gift for pianoforte effects and technical feats similar to Liszt's, though on a smaller scale. His style was brilliant, but much quieter, and his compositions were proportionately tamer than Liszt's. They are, indeed, more considerable in quantity than quality, though some of his studies are happily conceived and refined in style. He died at Naples in 1871.

Of far more poetical and real musical temperament was Adolf Henselt, who was born at Schwabach, in Bavaria, in 1814. He was a pupil of Hummel, and became a very considerable pianist in his early years. He played with great success in St. Petersburg in 1838, and was made Court pianist, and that capital became his home from that time till his death in 1888. He had a distinctly individual way of treating his instrument, both as composer and performer; obtaining great effects of sonority without vehemence, through the actual fulness and spread of his harmony and the genial warmth of his ideas. His works are few, confined to two books of Etudes and some lyrical pieces and a concerto. As a warm admirer of Weber he devoted great pains to editing and adapting his instrumental works to the capacities of the modern concert pianoforte.

Stephen Heller was born in Pesth in 1815, and is one of the most widely popular of pianoforte composers. He combined a wealth of graceful, poetical, and refined ideas with a very considerable sense of finish and a capacity to knit little movements into compact unity. Without being great, he certainly occupies an honourable position in his own field. He settled in Paris in 1838, and rarely moved from there till 1888, when he died. His works are mainly Etudes of a not very advanced standard of difficulty, and collections of short pieces known as "Promenades d'un Solitaire," "Nuits blanches," &c.

Among representatives of instrumental music must also be counted William Sterndale Bennett, who was born in 1816, at Sheffield. He began his musical career as a choirboy in King's Chapel at Cambridge, and his conspicuous talents caused him to be sent to the Royal Academy of Music, of which he ultimately became Principal in 1866. He was an admirable and refined pianist, of a quiet school, and wrote a considerable quantity of delicate and artistic pianoforte music, including the Sonata called "The Maid of Orleans," in which a programme is very definitely indicated. His works on a larger scale comprise some poetical Overtures, such as "Parisina," "The Wood Nymph," and "Paradise and the Peri," and an effective Concerto for pianoforte. He was one of the first Englishmen in modern times to develop any sense for orchestration. He died in 1875.

A conspicuous composer in all branches of instrumental music was Joachim Raff, born at Lachen, in Switzerland, in 1822. He began life as a schoolmaster, and was a man of culture and considerable general knowledge. Mendelssohn happened to take note of his musical talents, and recommended him to the famous publishers, Messrs. Breitkopf and Härtel. From 1850 onwards he enjoyed a remarkable degree of popularity all over Europe. He had a certain fund of poetry and romantic feeling, considerable instinct for effect, and extraordinary facility. He was a good deal in contact with Liszt, who was kind and helpful to him, and he avowedly allied himself with what was considered the advanced school of those days. He was fond of giving names to his works, and endeavouring to treat them as poems. Of his ten symphonies several bear distinctive names, such as "Im Walde," "Lenore," "Frühlingsklänge," "Im Sommer"; but in reality they do not break away from the traditions of sonata form in any very marked degree. His orchestration is effective and full of colour, and in many works of different types the texture is rich and elaborate, as, for instance, in his violin sonatas. His works in general show considerable gifts of invention, but are very unequal, both in style and intrinsic value. He died in 1882.

Anton Rubinstein, the most poetical and imaginative of modern pianists, was born in 1830, in a South-Western province of Russia. He began playing in public very early, and has spent great part of his life in concert tours. He did his own country special service by the foundation of the Conservatoire of St. Petersburg, of which he was principal for some time after 1862. He is a most prolific composer in every branch of art, and gifted with genuine musical ideas. One of his chief characteristics is impetuosity, and it is possibly owing to this circumstance that he is more successful in ideas than in construction. His work resembles in those respects the literature of his great fellow-countryman, Tolstoi. Indeed, it seems to be the rule with the artistic work of Slavs that the power of creating intrinsic interest is considerable, but that the faculties which are needed for concentration and systematic mastery of balance of design are proportionately weak. This is equally true of the very national composer, Tschaikowsky (born 1840), whose gifts have been exercised with characteristic results in concertos and other forms of instrumental art. Mention should also be duly made of the Russian composer Borodin (born 1834), who illustrates the same impetuous ardour, combined with a sense for technical feats in pianoforte playing of the same brilliant and surprising order as Liszt's.

The one great representative of the highest forms of instrumental music still living is Johannes Brahms, born in 1833 in Hamburg. He was introduced to Schumann by Joachim in 1853, and Schumann at once saw how great were his musical gifts and character, and wrote an enthusiastic article in the *Neue Zeitschrift für Musik* (in 1853), proclaiming him to the world as the man music was waiting for. However, the austerity and sternness of his musical character caused the public to be very slow in recognising him, though he had for constant champions such great exponents as Madame Schumann and

Joachim. Brahms has no sympathy with the methods of
the modern music-drama, or with the theories of composers
who attempt to apply those methods to instrumental music.
He is at once a musical intellectualist and a man of powerful
and concentrated feeling. He seems to judge instinctively
that self-dependent music is artistically intelligible only on
grounds of design and development; and he applies all the
artistic resources which the long period of musical development has made possible to the expounding of his musical
ideas in lofty and noble symphonies, and in splendid examples
of all kinds of chamber music, such as Pianoforte Quintets
and Quartets, Trios, String Quintets and Quartets, and other
combinations of solo instruments. It must be confessed that
his powers are so great that he still finds how to do something
new and individual in the old forms of the sonata order. He
did not attempt Symphonies till comparatively late in life,
No. 1, in C minor, being Op. 68, and the date of its appearance
1876, though it was actually written much earlier. The
second, in D, followed in 1877, and a third and fourth in F
and E minor have followed in recent years, as well as two
fine and very difficult Concertos for pianoforte, and one Violin
Concerto, and one double Concerto for violin and cello,
and two Overtures. His treatment of the orchestra is
austere but powerful; as though he disdained the subtle
seductions of colour, and used only such grave and almost
neutral tints as befitted the self-contained dignity of his
ideas. He obviously eschews programme even in pianoforte
pieces; but his numerous Capriccios, Intermezzos, Ballades,
and Rhapsodies are as full of genuine impulse as the best
works of the programme composers, and are often very
original in design. He is also one of the few great masters
of the Variations form—which is one that only the very
greatest composers have excelled in—and has produced
superb examples for orchestra as well as for pianoforte.

The branching out into variety of style and method which
is so characteristic of the progress of music is illustrated
by the increase of the influence of various national styles
of expression upon notable composers. Hungarian music
led the way in this respect, and influenced Schubert as well
as Liszt and Brahms. Russian music followed, as above
indicated, and in later times Norwegian and Bohemian music
have come prominently forward. The former is conspicuously
illustrated in the person of Edward Grieg, born at Bergen
in 1843. He has adopted in all his compositions certain

fantastic and piquant traits of harmony, rhythm, and melody, which appear to be drawn from the national style of his country. He has a very happy gift for knitting his little lyrical movements into compact and deftly finished wholes, and his sense for effect both with pianoforte and orchestra is very keen. Though the intellectual processes of concentrated development are not much in his line, the piquant novelty of his diction has gained also for his Violin Sonatas and for his Pianoforte Concerto a wide popularity.

Bohemian music is represented by Antonin Dvořák, who was born in 1841 at Mühlhausen, near Kralup, where his father was butcher and innkeeper. He played in town bands, and in the National Theatre at Prague, and did not come into public notice as a composer till comparatively late. But when once started, about 1877, his progress to world-wide fame was very rapid. He has written several admirable symphonies, and a great deal of fine and interesting chamber music. He is generally at his best in the national style, which is his true sphere; as in the "Furiants" and "Dumkas," which he sometimes introduces into his instrumental works in the position usually occupied by Scherzos and slow movements; and in the expression of such romantic folk-stories as "The Spectre's Bride," and in the superb sets of "Slavische Tänze." He is one of the greatest masters of orchestration living; and though in mastery of design and consistency of style he is a little uncertain, the profusion and freshness of his ideas place him very high in the ranks of living composers.

Of composers who have done honourable and skilful work in the instrumental lines there are in modern times too many even to catalogue. The above have so far made most mark upon history, and can only be supplemented by reference to names of such high distinction as Niels Gade, the Dane (born 1817), Max Bruch (born 1838), an admirable master of choral as well as instrumental effect, and the writer of very popular violin concertos; Karl Reinecke (born 1827), the present director of the Gewandhaus Concerts at Leipzig, and a prolific and successful composer; Felix Draeseke, a composer gifted with highly original and romantic ideas (born 1835); Xaver Scharwenka, a very successful composer of artistic pianoforte music (born 1840); Johann S. Svendsen, the Swedish composer of overtures, symphonies, and chamber music (born in Christiania in 1840); the admirable organist and writer of organ and chamber music, Joseph Rheinberger (born 1859); the popular composer of brilliant pianoforte music, Moritz Moszkowski (born 1840); the highly gifted but unfortunately short-lived Hermann Goetz (born 1840, died 1876); the Polish born Jean Louis Nicodé, a very highly gifted composer of instrumental music of various kinds (born 1853); and the English born Eugene d'Albert, who is one of the finest pianists of the age, and possessed of very high gifts as a composer (born at Glasgow, 1864).

In France, pure instrumental music has never been cultivated, but a few of her composers have written some effective music, mostly of a light and unclassical character; amongst others, Delibes (born 1836), who wrote such charming ballet music as the "Coppelia" and "Sylvie"; Lalo (born 1823), who has written chamber music, and a very effective Violin Concerto, as well as orchestral music; Saint-Saëns (born 1835), who has attacked classical forms of art in an unusually serious mood for a Frenchman. Italy is mainly represented by Sgambati, a pupil of Liszt's (born 1843), who has written much effective chamber music and other instrumental music including two symphonies. The natural field for English composers seems to be choral music, but instrumental music has also thriven remarkably well of late in the hands of such composers as Mackenzie (1847), Stanford (1852), Cowen (1852), Cliffe (1857), and several younger composers.

CHAPTER XI.

MODERN OPERA.

THE composers of Italian Opera after Gluck's time, unaffected by his exhortations to reform, continued to concentrate their efforts on pleasing their audiences. In this direction they succeeded extremely well. The most conspicuous proof of the fact was the career of Gioachino Rossini, born at Pesaro near Ancona in 1792. His father's circumstances were comparatively low and his own opportunities of musical education rather slender. He earned a little money as a boy by singing; was admitted into the Lyceum at Bologna in 1807, learned some counterpoint, and wrote his first opera, "La Cambiale di Matrimonio" (the Marriage Market), for Venice in 1810. He followed it up with a number of light comic operas in similar style, and won his first great success in opera seria with "Tancredi" in 1813. The music, though often borrowed from familiar sources, exactly hit the taste of typical opera audiences, and from that time what is known as the Rossini fever began, and spread by degrees over the greater part of Europe. Several buffa operas followed "Tancredi," and he had one or two checks before he arrived at the full measure of his popularity. "L'Italiana in Algeri," produced in Venice in the same year as "Tancredi," was a success, "Aureliano" was a failure, so was "Torvaldo e Dorlinska," and so at first was the famous "Barbiere." But this last failure was merely owing to the fact that the Romans, for whom it was written, were much attached to a setting by Paisiello, and regarded it as an impertinence of the young composer to use the same subject. In the end the superior *verve* and tunefulness of Rossini's work won its way, and it still holds a prominent place in the class of opera buffa. His next important opera seria was "Otello," which came out at Naples in 1816, and the rest of his most successful works in the purely Italian style consisted of the opera buffa "Cenerentola" (Rome, 1817), "Gazza Ladra" (Milan, 1817), "Mosè in Egitto," a sort of dramatic oratorio (Naples, Lent, 1818), "Ricciardo" (Naples, 1819), "Ermione" (1819), "Donna del Lago" (Naples, 1819), "Bianca e Faliero" (Milan, 1819), "Maometto Secondo" (Naples, 1820), "Zelmira" (Naples, 1820), "Semiramide" (Venice, 1823). The facilities for producing operas in

Naples were brought to an end in 1820 by an insurrection which got rid of the King, and at the same time reduced the resources of the famous opera manager Barbaja, who had hitherto combined the operatic business with the farming of gambling houses. Rossini, therefore, was induced to go to Vienna, and " Zelmira " was written with more care than usual, with a view to performance there. In 1823 he came to London, under contract with the manager of the King's Theatre, Benelli, to produce a new opera. He was extravagantly *fêted*, and made a large sum of money by playing the accompaniments for singers at fashionable parties for £50 a night; but the opera manager failed, and his new opera was never completed. He then went to Paris, where all the world again fell at his feet; and fortunately the Parisian traditions of French opera, which had always kept the dramatic elements well in sight, influenced him very happily. He began his career there with old works refurbished, some of them with new names. "Maometto" appeared again as "Le Siége de Corinthe," and "Mosè in Egitto" was revised as "Moïse." His most important work, "Guillaume Tell," with libretto by Scribe, was produced at the Académie in 1829, and it was his last. The superior type of audience he addressed in Paris made him more careful, and the result showed how great his powers were in all directions, in respect of orchestration as well as mere vocal effect. Even the style is more genuine and sincere than in his earlier productions. But he went no farther. It may have been his notorious indolence of disposition or jealousy of Meyerbeer. He lived till 1868, worshipped by society till the last, but without writing anything more except some small fugitive pieces and a mass.

It is greatly to his honour that he appreciated Mozart and Haydn. His ardour for their music in his youth caused him to be called " il Tedeschino "—the little German. Their influence upon his work is conspicuous in all its better aspects and also in his use of their melodic phrases. He was much better and more artistic in his orchestration than other Italians, and was distinctly inventive in the matter of effect. He deserves credit for trying to improve the treatment of the ordinary parts of the dialogue, and for making the recitative musically a part of the work, as Mozart had often done. Whatever his shortcomings, he towered over most of his compatriots in the following generation both in ability and artistic sincerity.

His contemporary, Mercadante (born 1797), was very popular in Italy. He was educated at Naples, and wrote both buffa and serious operas, such as "Elisa e Claudio" (1822), "Il Giuramento" (1837). He died blind in 1870. Donizetti (1798—1848), following Rossini's lines without his higher gifts, had great success with "Anna Bolena" (1830), "L'Elisire d'Amore" (1832), "Lucrezia Borgia" (1834), "Lucia di Lammermoor" (1835), "Favorita" and "Fille du Regiment" (Paris, 1840), "Don Pasquale" (Paris, 1843). He was educated at the Conservatorio at Naples, and paid much attention to solo singing of the tuneful order, and was consequently very popular with opera singers as well as their audiences; and he had the advantage of being interpreted in his time by the finest singers in the world, such as Grisi, Rubini, Tamburini, Lablache, and Mario.

Bellini, born at Catania in Sicily (1802), was also educated at Naples, and learnt early to concentrate his attention upon the requirements of solo singers; and they were consequently much at his service. The first of his operas to make any mark was "La Pirata" (1827), which was written under the actual supervision of the famous tenor Rubini, who sang in it with immense success. "Sonnambula" came out in 1831, at the Scala in Milan; "Norma" in 1832, "Puritani" in 1835. He died in the latter year.

Guiseppe Verdi was born at Roncole in 1813, where his father was an innkeeper. He had very slender opportunities to cultivate music till his eighteenth year, when he went to Milan and studied energetically for a time and learnt to appreciate Mozart's music. His first public appearance as an opera composer was with "Oberto" (1839). "Proscritto" followed in 1844, and was better known later under the name of "Ernani"—the name of the famous play by Victor Hugo. His fame grew by degrees and he took an important position as an opera composer of better stamp than the immediately preceding Italian composers, with "Rigoletto"—founded on Victor Hugo's impressive play "Le Roi s'amuse"—in 1851. "Trovatore" and "La Traviata" followed in 1853, "Vespri Siciliani" (1855), "Ballo in Maschera" (Rome, 1857), "Don Carlos" (Paris, 1867). These were mainly of the class popular with fashionable opera audiences, though they contain much skilful work, such as the famous quartet in "Rigoletto," where the characters are kept very clearly distinct. The influence of the sincerer type of German art began to tell upon him as time went on, and its effect is shown in "Aïda," written for the Viceroy of Egypt for performance at Cairo, in 1871. The same influence, and that of his friend Boito, are even more apparent in his recent "Otello," which is eminently dramatic, and shows his great powers in all branches of musical effect alike, especially in dramatic expression. His latest work, "Falstaff," which came out in February, 1893, exhibits the traces of the same happy influences.

In France, in recent times, the fruits of the national instinct for the stage have been most happily shown in operatic comedies and light comic operas. These branches of opera originated from the Italian opera buffa which made its appearance in Paris a little before Gluck's time. The French composers imitated and improved upon it. Their natural wit, sense of finish and neatness, and lightness of skilful handling, all found a most suitable province for exercise, and the result in the hands of the later composers is singularly artistic and good of its kind.

One of the most successful of the early representatives of this kind of art was Boieldieu, born at Rouen in 1775. He began his career in Paris in 1797, with the opera "La Famille Suisse." Among his chief successes was "Le Calife de Bagdad," which came out in 1800. The most famous of all was "La Dame blanche" (1825), which has had the most pronounced success of any opera of its kind. The thousandth performance was celebrated in 1862. It appears to be still alive in France at the present day. Boieldieu himself lived only till 1834.

Auber, whose successes are of a wider scope, and whose artistic powers were of a much higher order, was born at Caen in 1784. He began as an amateur, and was for a time a clerk in an office in London. He began composing little operas for Parisian theatres in 1811. Associated with the brilliant librettist Scribe, he came more into prominence with "Leicester" (1822), "Le Maçon" (1825), "Fra Diavolo" (1830), and "Les Diamants de la Couronne" (1841). The greater part of his work belongs to this light class of French opera comique, of which it is most brilliantly representative. His one serious opera, "Masaniello," or "La Muette de Portici," also had very conspicuous success. It came out in 1828, and made a great impression on quite different grounds from his lighter works; as he proved himself to have great dramatic powers, and used his orchestral forces for such purposes well. The opera had the singular honour of precipitating a popular revolution in Brussels, in 1830. Auber lived till after the German siege of Paris. The horrors of the Commune are reported to have hastened his end, which happened in 1871.

Another more short-lived composer of this light kind of opera was Hérold, born in Paris in 1791. He wrote much popular music for the pianoforte, and ballet music, and many operas, solid as well as light. The most famous were "Zampa" (1831) and "Le Pré aux Clercs (1832). He died in 1833 of consumption. Halévy, whose original name was Levi, was born in 1799. He also wrote various operas of diverse calibres. The best of his grand operas were "La Juive" (1835) and "La Reine de Chypre" (1841). They both show considerable sense of effect and skill of orchestration. Among his comic operas, "L'Eclair" (1835) was notable. He was also remarkably successful in ballet music. He died of consumption, like Hérold, in 1862.

The impulse towards scenic display, which was always liable to become prominent in French opera, even in Lulli's time, and is peculiarly noticeable in the works of Spontini and Halévy, came to a head in the works of Meyerbeer. This famous composer, whose real name was Meyer Beer, was the son of a German banker in Berlin, where he was born in 1791. He was extraordinarily clever in many ways, for in early years he was chiefly famous for his brilliant abilities as a pianist and for his remarkable gift for reading from score. He was a pupil of Vogler simultaneously with Weber, and began his career as an opera composer with some German operas, which were not successful. After that he went to Italy and produced a great number of operas in a regular Italian style (much to his friend Weber's regret), and won considerable success. He also tried a combination of Italian and German styles in "Il Crociato in Egitto" ("The Crusader in Egypt"), which came out in 1826 in Paris. His coming into contact with Parisian tastes turned his views in a new direction. The susceptibilities of the French to imposing spectacular display possibly indicated to him that they would be just the audience for gifts of his order. He studied French character and history carefully, and, with the congenial assistance of the librettist Scribe, made his first venture in the new line with "Robert le Diable," in 1831. He had calculated so well that the result gave him at once a commanding European reputation. He was very cautious and slow in maturing his work, calculating and testing his effects with infinite patience, and his successive operas therefore came far apart. " Roberto " was followed by " Les Huguenots " in 1836, " Le Prophète " in 1849, having been finished as early as 1843 but kept back; " L'Etoile du Nord " came out in 1854, " Dinorah " in 1856. " L'Africaine " was kept by him for over twenty years, as he never could finally satisfy himself that he had got it all sufficiently up to his idea of effect. It was not performed till 1865, two years after his death (1863).

Meyerbeer tried many styles and won popular favour in more than one, but it is as a representative of French grand opera that he is specially known to fame. He had great sense of theatrical effect without much real dramatic power. His operatic work dazzles and astonishes the senses, but does not appeal to deeper feelings or express any noble emotion. He carried the French taste for display to a climax and surpassed everyone who preceded him in supplying fit music for crowded scenes and pompous spectacles. He wielded great resources with remarkable success, and used all the old conventions of arias, flourishes, and set movements without scruple; and, taken altogether, his work is the hugest pile of clever artificial emptiness which exists in the whole range of music.

Of very different calibre is Gounod, who was born in 1818. His genuine sensibility is conspicuous, and his feeling for beauty of orchestral colour, and even for choral effect at times, is remarkable. He studied at the Conservatoire in Paris under Halévy. Going to Rome in 1839 he became enamoured of the old ecclesiastical style for a time. Then he fell in love with German music and Berlioz, and the latter exercised a very permanent influence upon him. He has won great and eminently deserved success in both kinds of opera. His lighter operas are worthy of association with the best types of this admirable branch of French art; and his great success in grand opera with " Faust," for which he had to wait so long, is too familiar to need comment. In this last the wholesome influence of German romanticism is clearly displayed, and his efforts in the direction of genuine expression are as conspicuous in his best works as they are conspicuously absent from Meyerbeer's productions. " Sapho " was his first opera (1851), and the most important of those which succeeded it are " La Nonne sanglante " (1854), " Le médecin malgré lui " (1858), " Faust " (1859), " Philemon et Baucis" (1860), "La Reine de Saba" (1862), "Mireille" (1864), "Romeo et Juliette" (1867), "Polyeucte" (1878).

Among the many successful representatives of modern French opera of various kinds, the following also deserve honourable recognition. Lalo (born at Lille, 1823), whose comprehensive powers have been referred to above in connection with instrumental music, has also produced considerable impression with his "Roi d'Ys." Delibes (born 1836), whose brilliant gifts have been most effectually shown in ballet music, has also been very successful in the line of opera, especially in "Le roi l'a dit" (1873) and "Lakmè" (1883). Bizet, whose characteristic and dramatic "Carmen" has given him such world-wide fame, was born in Paris in 1838. He studied at the Conservatoire, and wrote several operas which were not very successful till "Carmen," which was his last, and came out in 1875, in which year he died. The remarkable instinct for effect possessed by Massenet has brought him into considerable prominence as a representative of modern French tendencies. His most celebrated operas are "Don César de Bazan" (1872), "Le roi de Lahore (1877), the semi-religious opera "Herodiade" (1881), "Manon" (1884), "Le Cid" (1885). A composer of remarkable gifts is Alexis Chabrier (born 1841), who has produced several operas, such as "Gwendoline" (1886) and "Le roi malgré lui" (1887). The operatic works of Ambroise Thomas (born at Metz, 1811), such as "Mignon" (1866) and "Hamlet" (1868) are well known; and so were some of the very numerous productions of Offenbach (born 1819) till recently. Among the most recent composers of French opera Messager is a happy representative. His "Basoche" is a very refined, artistic, and genial example of its class.

While France and Italy were already busy producing numbers of operas of all kinds, the Germans were still looking for the type of opera which should adequately represent the high standard of their taste and musical intelligence. After "Zauberflöte" a considerable time elapsed without any noticeable achievement, till Beethoven had at last found a subject which satisfied his scrupulous taste, and brought out "Fidelio" in 1805. In the interim since the "Zauberflöte" a good deal of progress had been made in orchestral art and in the development of the resources of expression. Beethoven himself had written his first three symphonies and a large number of sonatas, and the whole development of his first period lay behind him, so that "Fidelio" represents a very much more modern type of expression than Mozart's work. The treatment of the orchestra is much more rich and copious in variety, and the quality of the melody much less formal. As might be expected, the scenes which are best, musically, are those in which there is a great deal of real human feeling, as in the prison scene. In parts like the duet between *Marcellina* and *Jacquino,* and in *Rocco's* song, the traces of the old traditional operatic style are more apparent. As a whole the standard is too high for average operatic audiences, and this, joined with the fact that when the opera was first brought out in Vienna in November, 1805, the Austrians had just suffered serious reverses at the hands of the French, who were even in occupation of the city, caused the opera to be but a moderate success. After three performances it was laid aside till May, 1806, and then again till 1814, when it was produced in a considerably revised state. It won its way slowly in Europe, but has never had any popular success, though to intelligent musicians it represents the highest standard of noble art that has ever been put into an opera. "Fidelio," however, did not finally solve the problem of national opera, for though written to German words and of the lofty type consistent with the dignified attitude of Germans towards music, the subject is not German, and the music still has touches of the earlier manner, and is not distinctly Teutonic throughout.

Neither did Spohr, with the most excellent purposes, completely satisfy German aspirations, as his dramatic sense was much too limited. He had good opportunities for studying operatic requirements, as he had great experience of orchestral matters, and was appointed Conductor of the Vienna Opera House for a time in 1812. But his strong impulse towards music of the classical type, like sonatas and concertos, prevented his hitting the right vein in operas. The first which he brought to successful performance was "Der Zweikampf mit der Geliebten," or "The Lovers' Duel," which came out at Hamburg in 1810. The most notable of those which succeeded were "Faust" (completed 1813, performed at Prague under Weber in 1816), "Zemir und Azor" (1818), and "Jessonda" (1823). The latter was far the most successful of all, and indeed was highly appreciated in Germany for the excellent use of artistic resources and the generally pleasant texture of the whole. He wrote several more, but none of them are of any real dramatic importance.

The composer with whom the solution of the problem of National Teutonic Opera is always associated is Weber. The circumstances of his early years were not very promising, but his father's aspiration to have a prodigy producing operas in childhood, at least afforded him early experience of theatrical work. The son was drilled with the view of pushing him rapidly forward by Vogler, and produced his first opera, "The Dumb Girl of the Forest," at the age of fourteen. After that he was made a secretary at the Court of the King of Wurtemberg at Stuttgart, and when that part of his career was unexpectedly and abruptly closed, he resumed the occupation of music and went for concert tours round Germany as a pianist, his gifts in that line being very remarkable. He was first prominently touched by the national spirit when aspirations for independence seized on the Germans after Napoleon's conspicuous failure in the expedition to Moscow. Weber's own enthusiasm was expressed in his splendid national songs and part-songs to Körner's words, in the sets of the "Leyer und Schwert," which went the length of the land. He was further identified with national things through being appointed to organise a really German opera, first at Prague in 1813 and then at Dresden in the following year, where hitherto Italian opera had had a monopoly. And, finally, his Teutonic impulse found its full expression in the opera "Der Freischütz," which came out in Berlin in 1821. This, at last, was German work through and through. The style is the style of "Volkslieder" expanded so as to meet the requirements of the situation. The traces of Italian traditions have at last evaporated, and all is genuinely Teutonic, in subject and treatment alike. Moreover, the treatment is of the highest artistic quality. The orchestration was the finest and the most perfectly adapted for such purposes hitherto seen; the musical characterisation of the various actors in the drama is singularly clear and happy; and the expression is of that warm and sincere kind which essentially distinguishes the German style from that of all other nations. The dialogue is still spoken, as was traditional in the earlier German forms, such as the "Singspiel"; but the continuous texture of the ultimate type of Wagner is prefigured in many parts of the work, especially in the long scene allotted to *Agatha*, the heroine; in which many different divisions in different times and different moods are knitted together into an admirable unity.

In Weber's next important opera, "Euryanthe," which came out in Vienna in 1823, the dialogue was set as well as the more important parts of the work, and in some respects it rises to higher levels than "Der Freischütz." But the libretto itself is so foolish that it has prevented its having general success.

Weber's last opera, "Oberon," was written by invitation for England. It is a fairy play, and not much more fortunate in respect of the libretto than "Euryanthe." Weber came over to England to launch it, already in a broken state of health. He lived to see the first few successful performances, and had just made up his mind to return to his family in Germany on June 6, when on the morning of June 5 he was found dead in his bed in Sir George Smart's house. Wagner only expressed the general feeling when in the year 1844, on the removal of his body to Germany for reburial in Dresden, he described him as the most German of composers. The vices and virtues of his manner are alike German. His style is saturated with the Teutonic spirit. Even the vagueness and irregularity of his form in instrumental music come from his aspiration after expression, which from the first had been the conspicuous aim of Germans.

His style had much effect upon German composers generally, even outside operatic work, as, for instance, on Mendelssohn. Marschner (1796—1861) was also much influenced by him, and most naturally so, as he was associated with him for some time in the opera work at Dresden. He produced several very successful operas, all rather in Weber's style, and some of them on the same supernatural lines which Weber liked. Among the best were "Der Vampyr" (1828), which had a great success, and even a long run in England; another was "Der Templer und die Jüdin," founded on Walter Scott's "Ivanhoe." His last was "Hans Heiling" (1833), which is considered his masterpiece.

Schubert also wrote some operas, but none of them ever took any hold of the theatre. His instinct was too essentially lyrical, and his susceptibilities too delicate for theatrical work. Schumann also made his effort in "Genoveva" (1850, Leipzig), which contains superb music, but does not apparently hit the standard of the stage; which, considering Schumann's introspective disposition, is not surprising.

Other German composers who did successful work for the stage are Kreutzer (1782—1849), who wrote "Das Nachtlager in Granada"; Lindpaintner (1791—1856), a good conductor, who wrote a great many solid operas; Lortzing (1803—1852), a composer of good light comic operas, such as "Czar und Zimmermann" (1837), "Wildschütz" (1842), "Undine" (1845), and many others; Nicolai (1810—1849), who wrote the admirably artistic and effective opera "Die lustigen Weiber von Windsor"; and Peter Cornelius (1824—1874), who identified himself with the "new German" movement of the days when Liszt was at Weimar, when Wagner's career was but beginning, and produced "The Barber of Bagdad," which was brought out by Liszt in 1859.

The composer on whom the influence of Weber and Beethoven was exerted with most important results was Richard Wagner. This last great representative of music-drama was born at Leipzig in 1813. His father died when he was but a few months old, and his mother was soon married again to an actor named Ludwig Geyer; so he was surrounded by theatrical influences from his childhood. He early showed a passion for things dramatic, such as Greek plays and Shakespeare, and attempted to write plays of very tragic cast himself. He heard Weber's works in Dresden and learnt to worship them and Beethoven's symphonies. He began his actual career in 1833 as a chorus-master at a theatre in Würzburg, where an elder brother was engaged as an actor. After this he was successively conductor at the theatres of Magdeburg, Königsberg, and Riga. In these early years he wrote several operas in different styles, none of which were successful; and finally determined to try his fortune at the Paris Opera House, which was then regarded as the centre of the operatic world. As Meyerbeer's influence was paramount there he wrote his first grand opera, "Rienzi," very much in Meyerbeer's manner, with every kind of resource he could think of which ministered to spectacular and sensational effect. But, unfortunately, though he got an introduction from Meyerbeer to the director of the opera house, he never succeeded in getting a hearing for it. The only work of his which was heard by the Parisians was the libretto for his opera "The Flying Dutchman," which the opera manager took and gave to one of his band to set, and then performed that setting, but not Wagner's. After waiting for a long while, and enduring many privations and disappointments, Wagner had to give up all hope of a hearing in Paris. Ultimately "Rienzi" was accepted at

Dresden and performed there in 1842, and met with success; and it was followed after a little while by his appointment as conductor there. His own setting of "The Flying Dutchman" then obtained a hearing, but did not meet with so much success as "Rienzi." The latter had been more in the style people were accustomed to, and the pomp and display dazzled them, while "The Flying Dutchman" was more of the real Wagner, extremely dramatic, and unlike the familiar operas of either Italian or French pattern, and people were too much puzzled by it to enjoy it. In the end its great dramatic power, and the genuine interest of the story, as well as the very striking and characteristic music, have won it a firm position, and it is recognised as the first of Wagner's works which approximately represent him. Wagner realised the advantage of using traditional stories and national legends as the basis of his works, since they necessarily represent things out of the range of common everyday experience, and are free from the hackneyed associations which make the singing of dialogue (except in comic scenes) seem ridiculous.

He also realised that it was an advantage to choose subjects which were of special Teutonic interest—and the next he undertook after "The Flying Dutchman" was "Tannhäuser," the story of the Hill of Venus; he completed it by 1844 and brought it out in the next year. Being still more uncompromising than the previous opera it was not received with favour; to his great surprise, since he himself did not realise that his methods would be so unintelligible to minds accustomed to conventional things. However, he was not the man to go back or write at a lower level to please a public, and went on with "Lohengrin" and completed it in 1846. Unfortunately, in 1849 he was implicated in certain revolutionary proceedings in Dresden, and had to escape to avoid imprisonment. He fled to Liszt at Weimar first and thence to Paris. This episode caused him to lose his appointment at Dresden, and he had to remain in exile from Germany for many years. Liszt meanwhile, with the ardour which characterised him, was bringing out all sorts of operas of special interest at Weimar, and among them produced "Tannhäuser," soon after Wagner's flight, and then "Lohengrin" for the first time, also in 1852. Wagner himself never heard the latter till many years later.

During his exile Wagner mainly lived at Zurich in Switzerland. He occupied himself with much literary work, which caused him to consider the possibilities of the music-drama more carefully. He also took up the earliest forms of the myths of the Nibelungs and the Gods of Walhalla, and the national hero *Siegfried*, which are embodied in Norse as well as ancient Teutonic legends; and finding them too rich in materials for one opera, he resolved on developing them into a great cycle of music-dramas, like the ancient trilogies of the Greeks. The first, which is a sort of preface to the series, is "Das Rheingold," which was completed in 1854. "Die Walküre" followed in 1856, "Siegfried" was not completed till 1869, and "Götterdämmerung" (the Dusk of the Gods) was only brought to perfection in 1874. This series forms the group comprised under the general name "Der Ring des Nibelungen" (the Ring of the Nibelung).

His work upon the great cycle was frequently interrupted. While he was still at work on the "Walküre" he received an invitation to conduct at the Philharmonic Concerts in London for the season of 1855. His reputation was at this time a very curious one; so few people understood his music that his determination to be true to himself and act according to his convictions appeared like a sort of lunacy of conceit, and his energy to be the mere self-assertion of a charlatan. It was impossible for his visit to this country to be anything but a mockery. He tried to insist upon some necessary reforms in the arrangements, and gave his full energies to making the performances as good as possible; but, of course, he was not invited again.

A more serious interruption followed. It dawned upon him while he was in the middle of "Siegfried" that it was already a long time since he had brought anything new before the public, and that it might be unwise to let the ten or twelve years pass before the whole of "the Ring" could be completed without showing any sign of continued activity. So he set to work on "Tristan und Isolde" and completed it before going farther with "the Ring." The poem was finished in 1857, and he worked on steadily till the whole was complete in 1859. After its completion he resolved to make a new assault upon Paris to try and get his works heard. He gave concerts there with excerpts from various works, and, finally, through some influence at Court, got "Tannhäuser" ordered for performance. Immense sums were spent on the preparation, and after 150 rehearsals it was received with a pandemonium of uproarious opposition got up by a Parisian clique which prevented its even being audible.

A turn of better fortune followed. He received permission to return to Germany, and about this time he took in hand the composition of the delightfully genial "Meistersinger von Nürnberg." But things had gone so hardly with him that he was on the verge of throwing up the struggle for good. Just at the right moment came a message from the young King of Bavaria, offering him a small but sufficient pension and a home in his dominions where he could go on with his work in peace. This was followed by more reassuring events. "Tristan" was performed at Munich in 1865 and "Die Meistersinger" in 1868. In 1872 he settled in Bayreuth, and the foundation of the great theatre was laid. He again took up the composition of the great trilogy, and when the whole thing was complete and the theatre finished it was performed for the first time in 1876. About that time he completed the poem of "Parsifal," and went on with the composition shortly afterwards, and finished this last of his great music-dramas in 1882. The first performances took place at Bayreuth in the same year. He did not long survive them, but died in Venice in 1883.

Wagner's impulse was at first mainly dramatic. His musical powers grew as his career proceeded and scarcely arrived at maturity till the beginning of "the Ring." His great advantage lay in his control of all the factors of operatic art—as he attained a high degree of mastery of dramatic, theatrical, and musical effect, and in his hands each served to enhance the effect of the others. His reforms consisted mainly in getting rid of the old formulas, such as arias, recitatives, finales, and all the set movements which disturbed and hindered the action; and in thus making each act continuous music throughout. He developed the principle of the *Leitmotif* to the fullest extent, giving a definite musical figure to each character and situation; and using the figures all through the orchestral part of the work, instead of the old formulas of accompaniment. He enlarged the bounds of tonality so as to give himself as much room for expression as possible, and developed the resources of effect in the orchestra to the utmost. His treatment of the voice was the natural outcome of modern musical development. He reserved the finer melodic phrases for the occasions when much expression was required, and treated the rest like the old declamatory recitative, but with richer accompaniment.

CHAPTER XII.

MODERN VOCAL MUSIC.

No branch of modern music is more characteristic or more illustrative of prevailing tendencies than the solo song, for none illustrates more clearly the relation between music and the thought expressed, or the aim of the musician to be guided by the idea rather than the conventions of classical form. The typical modern song has only become possible through the long development of the resources of art, and only through long experience and innumerable experiments have men learnt what to do and what not to do in dealing with a poet's language. Songs existed from the beginning of musical time; but until the beginning of this century they consisted either of regular definite tunes which had to be fitted to all the verses, whatever change of sentiment or accent occurred; or of formal consciously artistic products like opera arias. Many tendencies combined to bring about the close wedding of music to word and sentiment, which began to be adopted at the beginning of the present century. Gluck's theories had some influence, for they caused people to pay more attention to the meaning of the words and the declamation. The development of instrumental resources and of pianoforte technique put fresh powers in the hands of composers. Mozart and Haydn both approached to the ideal of modern song here and there, and Beethoven in several cases actually attained it. Weber, through his intense sympathy with the Teutonic Volkslied, likewise produced both in his operas and in separate songs perfect examples of the true modern song; but the first composer whose personality was specially expressed in this branch of art was Franz Schubert, and he consequently stands out as the first representative song composer of modern times. He was one of the most spontaneous and one of the least systematically educated of musicians; and his musical nature was particularly open to follow external impressions. Knowing very little of the theory of form made him particularly amenable to the guidance of a poet, and he seems to have written his songs under the immediate impulse which the poems he read produced in him. There was hardly any development of his powers in this respect, for some of his very finest songs were written in early years. "Gretchen am Spinnrade" was written when he was but seventeen (1814) and the "Erl-König" when he was eighteen (1815), "Schwager Kronos" and the "Wanderer" followed soon after. Throughout the whole of his life he poured out song after song, and it was more the chance of a poem coming in his way than any other consideration which led to a composition. The beautiful set of twenty called "Die schöne Müllerin" belongs to the year 1823, "Die junge Nonne" to 1825, "Sylvia" to 1826, the "Winterreise" to 1827, and "Liebesbotschaft" and "Der Doppelgänger" to the last year of his life, 1828. In all he wrote over 600, many of them long, rich, and deeply expressive works.

Scientific writers on music are fond of classifying songs into certain categories in accordance with the nature of the musical treatment. Thus a very simple song with a tune would be called "Volksthümlich"—that is, in the national or Folk manner; a song which is very carefully carried out in detail, the music following the sentiment throughout, would be called a "durchkomponirtes Lied"; and a narrative song, "Ballade," and so forth. Schubert, of course, had no idea of such classification. The poems suggested to his mind the method of treatment. If the words were simple, he was satisfied to write a tune with a simple accompaniment and repeat the same for different verses; if the words were subtle and intricate in meaning, he adopted a more subtly artistic way of dealing with the musical material; if he had to tell a dramatic story he made the voice part declamatory and put the illustrative effects into the pianoforte part. It is rare that the special methods indicated by the scientific analysts persist through a song. Even the simplest have neat turns of artistic finish and subtleties of suggestion in detail, the most richly organised often have passages of vocal tune, and in the ballad-like songs every means is used to convey the musical counterpart of the words. He uses realism, colour, striking harmony, polyphony, modulation, as well as melody to bring home the poet's meaning. Melody is relegated to its right place as only one of the factors of effect, and a great deal of his expression is produced by striking harmony and modulation. Under such conditions the old idea of song has become almost obsolete and the word " accompaniment " a misnomer. The modern type of song is a complete work of art of a much more highly organised character than the old type. Harmony is an immensely more powerful means of expression than melody, and in bringing it to bear as a factor in the art-form the pianoforte necessarily occupies a far more important place than it used to do. It is through the treatment of what is technically called the accompaniment that the effects of harmony, modulation, and the rest become possible, and the resources of the composer for intensifying the poet's meaning and faithfully following his artistic intentions are immensely enhanced.

Schubert's songs were very slow in winning popular acceptance. Their very perfections were regarded as utter extravagance at first, but by the present day the best examples are regarded as the complete solution of the problem of song and are the prototypes of all modern products of the kind.

It is not necessary to discuss the songs of distinguished composers who are not particularly identified with the department of song. Spohr and Mendelssohn wrote some pleasant songs, but they were not by nature song-writers, and the same may be said of a large majority of able and conscientious composers who have succeeded in other lines.

Of genuine song-writers since Schubert, Schumann is one of the foremost. His literary tastes and his poetical views on art were in his favour. He did not begin writing songs till after he had written a considerable portion of his best pianoforte music. In 1840, the year of his marriage, he suddenly threw himself with ardour into song-writing, and in one year produced over a hundred, comprising nearly all the best he composed. Schumann, like Schubert, adapted his methods to the poems he set. He was less happy than Schubert in the descriptive line, but he touched a deeper vein of emotion and reached a higher pitch of warmth in colour and expression. He is most notable for his faithfulness to the poet's declamation, and the intense sympathy with which he follows every turn of thought and feeling.

Among composers whose fame is mainly centred in songwriting is Robert Franz, who was born in 1815 at Halle. Without the warmth or *verve* of the two greater composers, he has won the affection of his fellow-countrymen by the faithful care and insight with which he follows the poet's meaning and diction—fitting his music close to every word. He died in 1892.

The greatest of modern song-writers is Johannes Brahms.

A set of his early songs was among the things which first attracted the attention of Schumann, and throughout his life he has been constantly pouring out songs of an infinite variety of style, and form, and calibre. In no department is he more thoroughly great. He is completely in touch with his poet, and applies his immense artistic resources to the ends of expression without a trace of superfluous artifice or pedantry. In later years he has simplified his methods of treatment considerably. The finest songs belong to his early days and middle age, but out of many volumes of songs there are very few that have not decided point and genuine merit of the true song order.

The feeling for song-writing increases as Music becomes more elastic and free in its adaptability to varieties of expression, and the number of genuine song-writers has of late become very large indeed. Among the most remarkable is Hugo Brückler (born 1845, died 1871), whose settings of the songs in Scheffel's "Trompeter von Säkkingen" are of a very high order. The Norwegian, Halfdan Kjerulf (born 1815, died 1868), has won a wide and well deserved popularity for refined expression and well varied songs. Rubinstein has shown a very exceptional gift for song-writing, and has produced some of the best examples of modern times; and Taubert, Lassen, Grieg, Dvořák, Jensen, and Henschel have all contributed their share.

The French conception of song is much more superficial than the German, and concentrates much more attention on the voice part. But they have an admirable literature of modern lyrics, and the foremost composers of the country have supplied the world with a vast collection of refined and pleasant settings of them. Berlioz stands at the head of these French song composers with very characteristic examples in the "Nuits d'Été" and various separate songs, some of which are speculatively treated, and interesting on that account, as being out of the common line. Of modern composers Gounod has been specially successful in this country as well as in France, and not far behind come F. David, Massenet, Godard, and Widor.

In this country song-writing reached, in the past generation, a pitch of degradation which is probably without inartistic parallel in all musical history. Mercantile considerations and the shallowness of average drawing-room taste produced a luxuriant crop of specimens of imbecility in which the sickly sentiment was not less conspicuous

than the total ignorance of the most elementary principles
of grammar and artistic construction, and of the relation of
musical accent to poetical declamation. In those days the
songs of Hatton (1809—1886), and of Sterndale Bennett,
and the early songs of Sullivan and those of F. Clay
(1840—1889), were honourably conspicuous for real artistic
quality and genuine song impulse. Fortunately the lowest
point appears to have been reached, and though there are a
good many representatives of the old school still active, the
present day is represented by mature masters of their craft
who can write real genuine songs; such as Mackenzie, Stanford, Cowen, and Maude Valérie White, besides a few young
composers, such as MacCunn and Somervell, who produce
songs as genuine and as beautiful as are to be found anywhere
in Europe. The impulse is certainly going in the right
direction, and if the public can be persuaded not to insist so
exclusively upon songs being either vulgar or trivial and
vapid, the future of English song will undoubtedly be such
as the nation may be proud of.

A branch of art which is most characteristically modern,
and seems to have a great deal of life in it, is the combination
of orchestra with choral music and solos, independent of the
stage, such as is familiar in modern oratorios, cantatas,
odes, and so forth. The collapse of oratorio after the
time of Handel and Bach was mainly owing to the spread
of Italian operatic taste, which had moved rapidly away
from choral music as soon as the Neapolitan School of
composers gained hold of the world, and cared for nothing
but solo singing of the formal aria type. The influence
of the *prima donna* was even more pernicious in the line
of oratorio than in opera, for chorus is truly an essential
of the latter form; and when chorus was reduced to the
minimum possible, that form of art collapsed. Indeed,
the Italian influence was fatal to serious and sacred music
all round, and it was only in Protestant countries that
the traditions of grand oratorio lingered on, and it was in
Protestant countries that the resuscitation was achieved. A
sort of forlorn hope in this dreary period is the work of Philip
Emmanuel Bach in that line. His two oratorios, "The
Israelites in the Desert" (1775) and "The Resurrection"
(1787), are both very interesting, and contain passages of
great beauty and vivid expression. It is noteworthy that
they foreshadow the very lines on which the resuscitation
was cast, as there is an unusual amount of orchestral work

in them, some of it very happily conceived. They also contain fine choruses, but the stiffness of the arias militates against their revival in modern times.

It was, indeed, the development of orchestration, and the splendid opportunities which the combination of orchestra and chorus affords to composers, which led to the revival. In old days the instrumental accompaniment was purely secondary and subservient. The development of orchestral style and effect doubled the resources of composers in such works as oratorios, and supplied them with a very interesting problem to solve. Mozart was in the forefront of the new movement with his "Requiem," which is the noblest and most sincere of all his works. It was not finished at his death in 1791, but was completed afterwards by his pupil, Süssmayer, from memory, and by repeating one of the first movements, and adding new music where necessary, in a way which does him very great credit.

The "Requiem" was soon followed by Haydn's "Creation," which forms a kind of landmark for the real commencement of the new movement. Haydn had been in England and had heard some of Handel's choral works for the first time in the last decade of the eighteenth century. Salomon had offered him an arrangement of Milton's "Paradise Lost" to set, and when he returned to Germany he had it revised and translated, and set it forthwith. It was first performed privately in the Schwarzenberg Palace in Vienna, in 1798, Haydn at that time being sixty-five years old. It spread with marvellous rapidity to all musical centres, and was received with special enthusiasm in England. He followed it up two years later with "The Seasons," which goes by the name of an oratorio and contains choruses, but is, for the most part, much too light and secular to accord with the usual idea of oratorios. The next work of the kind by a great master was Beethoven's "Christus am Oelberge," known in England as "The Mount of Olives" and sometimes as "Engedi." Here the resources of the orchestra are even more richly used than by Haydn, but the style is rather florid and operatic. It is a comparatively early work of the great master, as it came out in 1803.

The most prominent composer in the field in the early years of the present century was Spohr, the great violinist. He began composition with the view of suiting himself with concertos, and succeeded so well that his powers as a composer were soon much in demand. He was invited to compose an oratorio for the Fête Napoleon at Erfurt, in 1812, and for that occasion wrote his first version of "The Last Judgment," under the German name of "Das jüngste Gericht." He prepared himself deliberately by borrowing a copy of Marpurg's "Art of Fugue" from one of his own pupils and studying like a neophyte, and the result seems to have justified his labour at the time, though the oratorio in question is not one that is familiar. His great work in this line was "Die letzten Dinge," which is also well known in England as "The Last Judgment." This was produced in 1826. It is remarkable as the first oratorio which has the modern romantic character about it. There is a certain vein of poetry and a thoroughly modern colour throughout, which comes partly from Spohr's skilful orchestration and partly from his chromatic manner; which, however, is not quite so pronounced in this work as in many others—as, for instance, in his oratorio "Calvary," which came out in 1835. Spohr's last composition of this class was "The Fall of Babylon," which was written for the Norwich Festival of 1842.

Contemporary with Spohr was F. J. C. Schneider (1786—1853), who wrote fourteen oratorios between 1810 and 1838, which at the time had much popularity. The best is said to have been "Das Weltgericht"; another called "Sündfluth" was known in England as "The Deluge." Another composer who had very remarkable success for a time was Neukomm (1798—1858). He was a pupil of Michael and Joseph Haydn. His oratorios, "Mount Sinai" and "David," were much in vogue in England before Mendelssohn's "St. Paul" came out. They are not without artistic merits, though the treatment of the Commandments in "Sinai" is extremely funny. "David" was written for the Birmingham Festival of 1834. The advent of Mendelssohn caused Neukomm to disappear in the background. Mendelssohn brought the skill of a complete master of both orchestral and choral effect to bear upon oratorio. He began with "St. Paul," which was first performed at Düsseldorf in 1836, and was soon taken up in England. Its success naturally led to his seeking for another subject, and he finally settled on "Elijah." But before that came out the "Lobgesang" or "Hymn of Praise" was produced at Leipzig on the occasion of the celebration of the fourth centenary of the invention of printing. This work, so popular in England, combines the qualities of a symphony and of an oratorio, and very emphatically illustrates the value of the combination of orchestral and choral effect. The famous "Elijah" was completed in 1846, and first performed at Birmingham on August 26 in that year. Mendelssohn began another oratorio, "Christus," but died in 1847 before completing it. It seems to have been intended to have been on the lines of the typical "Passions" of J. S. Bach. The influence of this form is very prominent in all his works of this class. He had taken up Bach's "Matthäus Passion" as early as 1827 and gave in Berlin the first performance it had received out of Leipzig since Bach's death. Its remarkable scheme came upon the world like a novelty, and it exercised an influence upon Mendelssohn's mind which was most powerful for good. He seized upon the salient principles of the "Passion" type, such as the admixture of narrative, reflective and dramatic principles in the solo parts, the use of types of choruses which represent masses of people who are personally engaged in the action of the drama, and the types of reflective choruses which express the mood of the spectator, and he applied these and other features of the old form with the happiest results. "St. Paul" is the most nearly on the "Passion" lines of the two, but the influence of the type is strong in both of them.

About the end of Mendelssohn's time composers became very busy with oratorios and similar works. Schumann produced the "Paradise and the Peri" in 1843 and the "Faust" music in 1848. In France the movement was early and brilliantly represented by Berlioz's remarkable "Damnation de Faust" and "L'Enfance du Christ." H. H. Pierson's "Jerusalem" was brought out at the Norwich Festival of 1852. Sterndale Bennett's principal work, "The May Queen," came out at Leeds in 1858; and his "Woman of Samaria" in 1867. Sullivan brought out his "Prodigal Son" at the Worcester Festival of 1869, and his "Light of the World" at Birmingham in 1873; Macfarren his "John the Baptist" in 1873 and "Joseph" at Leeds in 1877, and both composers followed up their successes with more in the same line, the latest and most popular of its kind being Sullivan's "Golden Legend." For England also were written Gounod's highly coloured "Redemption" and "Mors et Vita." In Germany the highest standard of this type of art is represented by Brahms's "Schicksalslied," "Triumphlied," "Nänie," "Gesang der Parzen," and "Deutsches Requiem." Bohemia is well represented by Dvořák's beautiful "Stabat Mater," his picturesque "Spectre's Bride," "Ludmila," and the "Requiem." Denmark is represented by numerous works of the kind by Niels Gade (born 1817); Italy by Verdi's notable "Requiem" for Manzoni, and Mancinelli's "Isaiah"; and Belgium by Benoit's "Lucifer."

Choral music seems to thrive best in countries where independent democratic spirit is strong and tempered with common sense. England has always been happiest in such music, and it is most natural that this characteristic form of modern art should thrive in her soil. Her composers have been extremely active and extremely successful in this line of late. Indeed, in the past twenty years the standard of such work has risen to a truly surprising degree. The richness and variety, the poetry and masterly craftsmanship of such works as Mackenzie's "Rose of Sharon" and "Dream of Jubal," and Stanford's "Eden" and "Revenge" and "Voyage of Maeldune," mark an awakening in English art which is most hopefully significant.* These indeed stand out as landmarks of the time; and they are very worthily supplemented by many other fine works by the same composers, and by a flood of works by their fellow composers which are all honourably artistic, and many of very high excellence, either for orchestral effect or choral effect, or for both together—such as Stainer's "Daughter of Jairus" (Worcester, 1878), "St. Mary Magdalen" (Gloucester, 1883), and "Crucifixion" (1887), Lloyd's "Hero and Leander" (Worcester, 1884) and "Andromeda" (Gloucester, 1886), Corder's "Sword of Argantyr" (Leeds, 1889), Bridge's "Callirhoë" (Birmingham, 1888) and "Nineveh" (Worcester, 1890), Cowen's "Sleeping Beauty" (Birmingham, 1885) and "Ruth" (Worcester, 1887), Williams's "Bethany" (1889) and "Gethsemane" (Gloucester, 1892), MacCunn's "Lay of the Last Minstrel" and "Lord Ullin's Daughter," Gray's "Arethusa" (Leeds, 1892), and a great many others. The constant increase and improvement of the musical intelligence of choral societies all over the country invites good work on the part of composers; and undoubtedly good music wedded to good poetry makes an artistic combination as worthy of intelligent beings as any that exists.

---

* Any list of modern compositions of a high order of merit would be incomplete without mention of "Blest Pair of Sirens," "De Profundis," "Job," and "Judith," from the pen of the author of this Primer.—EDITOR.

For EU product safety concerns, contact us at Calle de José Abascal, 56–1°, 28003 Madrid, Spain or eugpsr@cambridge.org.

www.ingramcontent.com/pod-product-compliance
Ingram Content Group UK Ltd.
Pitfield, Milton Keynes, MK11 3LW, UK
UKHW041419180426
11947UKWH00007B/215